813

THE MURDER BOOK
*An Illustrated History
of the Detective Story*

THE
MURDE

Tage la Cour
and Harald Mogensen

R BOOK

An Illustrated History of the Detective Story

Translated from Danish
by Roy Duffell

GEORGE ALLEN AND UNWIN LTD
RUSKIN HOUSE   MUSEUM STREET   LONDON

ISBN 0 04 809003 4

Originally published as *Mordbogen.*
© 1969 Lademann Forlagsaktieselskab, Copenhagen.

Printed in Czechoslovakia

COVER PHOTOGRAPH: *Lennart Larsen*

END PAPERS: *Margaret Rutherford*
as Agatha Christie's Miss Marple (MGM)

TITLE PAGE VIGNETTE:
Drawing by unknown artist from
Cleveland Moffett's novel
Through the Wall

Contents

The father of the detective story: Edgar Allan Poe

Poe was born in Boston on 29 January 1809. His father, David Poe, had studied law at Baltimore, where he met a young English actress, Elizabeth Arnold. They ran away and got married, David becoming an actor and touring with his wife. Soon they had two children, Edgar being born a year after his brother, Henry. But a few months before the birth of their sister, Rosalie, David left his wife, and Elizabeth, already suffering from tuberculosis, died in poverty. Henry and Rosalie were looked after by relatives, but Edgar, still not three, was taken into the family of a wealthy business man, John Allan.

The Danish artist, Arild Rosenkrantz produced a great many illustrations for the two-volume Danish edition of Edgar Allan Poe's TALES OF MYSTERY AND IMAGINATION, *published in 1907–8, all of which succeeded in combining artistry with the macabre quality of the originals. The skull above is from* THE GOLD BUG.

The authentic atmosphere of Paris was captured by Charles Raymond Macauley, the American artist, in his illustrations for THE MURDERS IN THE RUE MORGUE *in the first annotated edition of three Auguste Dupin stories. This one shows Dupin and friend wandering through Paris by night while the amateur detective displays such astonishing analytical skill that his friend imagines he must be a thought-reader.*

Though Mr Allan was severe, his wife, Frances, adored Edgar. In 1815 the Allans took him on a long business trip to England, where they sent him to boarding school in Stoke Newington. The principal, the Rev. Dr Bransby, and his extraordinary establishment are decribed in Poe's short story, *William Wilson*. Five years later the family returned to America, where Poe continued his schooling. In 1826 he entered Virginia University, leaving at the end of the year of his own free will and not, as stated in many biographies, on account of gambling debts.

Poe's weakness for drink, no doubt inherited, caused Allan to wash his hands of him, and he had no other course than to enlist in the army. There he conducted himself well and succeeded in entering West Point Academy – only to be relegated later for neglect of duty. Meanwhile his foster mother lay dying in Richmond. Her last wish was to see Edgar again. But it was not to be. When Edgar finally heard of Frances Allan's death he returned home and spent several nights in vigil at her graveside.

For the next eight years he travelled restlessly. Meanwhile his stories were becoming increasingly popular. At the age of eighteen he had published *Tamerlane and Other Poems* under a pseudonym. Only seven copies of that edition now exist. Then in 1833, the year after his foster father died, leaving him nothing, he won the first prize of fifty dollars offered by a weekly for the best short story submitted. Gradually Poe's writings became so popular that the leading periodicals vied with each other for his work. But the money he earned melted like dew before the sun, and when, in 1836, he married his fourteen-year-old cousin, Virginia Clemm, he owned nothing. Virginia died of tuberculosis in 1847.

A Metro-Goldwyn-Mayer film of 1951, MAN WITH A CLOAK, *was about Poe and was based on John Dickson Carr's short story,* THE GENTLEMAN FROM PARIS. *Joseph Cotten is seen below in the leading role.*

Russell Hoban was rather more romantic in his approach than Arild Rosenkrantz. This water-colour for THE GOLD BUG *is from 1963.*

Again Poe was rootless, moving around in a constant alcoholic and narcotic haze. A young girl promised to marry him if only he would give up drink. Instead, Poe courted a married woman – until he met a childhood sweetheart, by then an elderly spinster. He proposed to her, but when she accepted him he set off on a fresh bout of drinking. One morning he woke to find himself in jail, although when the authorities learned his identity they immediately released him. Soon after, on 15 November 1849, after a violent attack of delirium tremens, he died in hospital.

How Poe hit on the idea of the 'detective story'

Edgar Allan Poe can claim the credit for writing the first detective story – incidentally, without once using the term 'detective'. The reason he was first in the field was simply that none of his predecessors in that macabre genre had any means of knowing about detectives. Until the hated police spies of the despots had been replaced by detectives as we know them now, it was impossible to romanticize their exploits into thrilling adventure stories. And so it was only natural that the detective story came into being about the middle of the last century – when the police were reorganized – and that it should have done so in three of the oldest democracies, the United States, France and England, for at its best democracy always upholds the rights of society and the individual.

On 1 April 1841 the Philadelphia periodical 'Graham's Magazine' published *The Murders in the Rue Morgue*. This story launched Poe's brilliant amateur detective, the Chevalier C. Auguste Dupin, who later performed with equal bravura in *The Mystery of Marie Rogêt* and *The Purloined Letter*. Add to these three Dupin stories *Thou art the Man!*, *The Gold Bug* and *The Man of the Crowd* and you have the five recipes on which nine-tenths of all subsequent detective stories have been based.

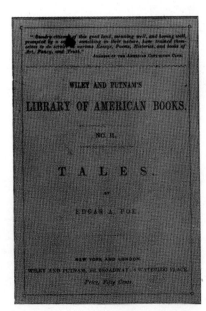

The roadside inn at Weehawken where Mary Rogers, accompanied by a young man of dark complexion, took some refreshment shortly before she was murdered.

In *Thou Art the Man*! the least likely person turns out to be the villain, although the present-day reader will have no difficulty in guessing the murderer and will find the whole story slightly naive. In *The Gold Bug* you have the romantic story of buried treasure on a secret island discovered by the detective, William Legrand, who deciphers a code that is incomprehensible to everyone else. *The Man of the Crowd* is a story of one man shadowing another, a feature that was later to become so popular, and it is interesting to note that this short work, after years of neglect, is now one of the most popular that Poe wrote.

Paris by night in the mid-nineteenth century, when Dupin lived there, was not pure idyll, and the Rue Morgue would have been much like the street depicted here.

Inspired by that hair-raising thriller, THE CASK OF AMONTILLADO, *Arild Rosenkrantz produced this illustration – gruesome enough for anyone's taste.* ▶

In *The Murders in the Rue Morgue* two women are brutally murdered in an apparently locked room. The suspect arrested by the police is innocent, and it is the amateur detective who succeeds in finding the solution to the mystery. Most readers probably know it already, so there will be no harm in revealing that Poe got the idea from what is said to be a true story of an orang-outang which had been trained to climb through windows and steal what it could find. This story was much discussed in 1834, and it is safe to assume that Poe had read it.

14

The Murders in the Rue Morgue and *The Mystery of Marie Rogêt*

Poe's second detective story, *The Mystery of Marie Rogêt*, appeared as a serial in three numbers of Snowden's 'The Lady's Companion' – those of November 1842, December 1842 and February 1843. It was the forerunner of the intellectual crime story. The author took an actual case of murder and reported it in slightly disguised form, adding his own comments. The real name of the Parisienne, the Marie Rogêt of the story, was Mary Cecilia Rogers, a flighty cigar-girl who was found murdered in the Hudson River on 28 July 1841. The murder had a number of curious features, all of which greatly interested Poe. But he allowed a year to pass before, well removed from the scene of the crime, he wrote the short story in which he claimed to solve a murder that had baffled the police. The truth, however, is that only the first five of the articles quoted by him had appeared in American papers; the sixth and vital one, which hints at a young naval officer as being the murderer, is pure fiction. Thus the whole basis of Poe's alleged solution falls to the ground – a fact which does not, of course, make the story any the less readable.

The Purloined Letter, Poe's third Dupin story, is artistically the best. It was first published in 'The Gift', the title page adding 'Philadelphia, 1845'. In fact this little New Year gift appeared at the end of 1844. It is the prototype story of the stolen document, the disappearance of which could cause the gravest international complications if it were to get into the wrong hands. Again the police are baffled, and our detective solves the mystery with the aid of his superior psychological insight and analytical skill.

Poe did not, of course, gain international literary fame solely on the basis of a few crime and detective stories. But through them he created, and left his mark on, the most popular genre in light literature.

THE MURDERS IN THE RUE MORGUE *was filmed in 1932 with Bela Logosi as a Hoffmannesque 'Dr Miracle' (left). In the Warner Bros version of 1954 Karl Malden played the part of Dupin (centre). The prison (right) where Poe spent a night in September 1849.*

Murder in the Far East

Ellery Queen's bibliography, *The Detective Short Story*, includes ten anthologies of Chinese short stories from the period between the seventh and eighteenth centuries. Apart, however, from Dr Herbert A. Giles's translation of 164 of the many hundreds of stories by Pu Sung Ling, which was published in Shanghai in 1908, they are either irrelevant to our purpose or printed only in Chinese. For many years readers in the western world have had to rely for knowledge of the Chinese detective story entirely on the work of the Sinologist and bibliophile, Vincent Starrett. In his long and detailed essay of 1942, *Some Chinese Detective Stories*, Starrett refers to such books as *The Exploits of Magistrate Pao* (Pao Kung An), *The Seven Heroes and the Five Just Men* (Ch'i Hsia Wu I), and *Curious Events in the Reign of Wu T'se T'ien* (Wu T'se Chin An), which glorify the exploits of two of China's most famous detectives, Dee Jendijeh and Pao Cheng, both of whom were magistrates. Their deductions are often the result of inspired guess-work, while, as in all Chinese folk literature, belief in the metaphysical plays an inevitable role. For this reason they are of less interest to the present-day reader as detectives. Part of the game is to know the villain from the start. The reader's enjoyment consists not in guessing or deducing the identity of the villain but in appreciating the genius of the detective as, step by step, he succeeds in unmasking the criminal.

In Pao Kung (Magistrate Pao) the Chinese had a hero to satisfy their sense of justice. And he really did at one time exist, having been the most famous magistrate at the time of Emperor Jen Sung. He died in 1062 and it used to be said of him, 'Magistrate Pao smiles when the Yellow River is clear', so he would hardly be called one of the jovial sort.

But in Vincent Starrett's opinion *The Exploits of Magistrate Pao* ranks after *Curious Events* as the most entertaining collection of stories. And on this point he and Dr van Gulik agree.

Magistrate Dee would stop at nothing to obtain a confession: torture, lies, and empty promises, while playing on his victim's fear of ghosts and underworld spirits. Old Chinese drawing.

Dr Robert van Gulik studied law and philology at the universities of Leyden and Utrecht, taking his doctor's degree in 1933. In the same year he became secretary at the legation in Tokyo, later serving in various missions in the Far East until he became ambassador to the Lebanon, and finally, in 1959, to Malaysia. Dr van Gulik had already written several books on Asian art, literature and history when, in 1949, he translated three Magistrate Dee murder mysteries entitled *De Goong An*, the translation being published in Tokyo. The book was too Chinese in character to interest the general reader and was only published privately for the benefit of orientalists and students of the history of the detective story.

Dee lived in the early seventh century in the reign of Empress Wu – an extraordinary ruler who was not only a strikingly beautiful courtesan but also a brilliant and witty woman, responsible for many beneficial and humane laws. The picture (right) shows Dee surrounded by his wives.

Magistrate Dee, Pao Kung and Edogawa Rampo

Robert van Gulik decided to try his hand at rewriting some of China's oldest detective stories to bring them more into line with present-day needs without spoiling their originality and charm. The result of his first effort was *The Chinese Maze Murders*, which first appeared in Chinese in Singapore in 1953, to be followed three years later by an English edition printed in Holland. Like all the succeeding stories the book is a Chinese puzzle, consisting of three mysteries, one inside the other: *The Murder in the Locked Room*, *The Concealed Will*, and *The Girl with the Missing Head*. The titles are reminiscent of Poe's three Auguste Dupin stories, but the plots come direct from ancient and medieval China, so there can be no question of plagiarism. They are further proof that there is nothing new under the sun. But the familiar can, of course, be served up in a wide variety of guises.

As a detective story *The Chinese Maze Murders* is too long-winded, and suffers from other blemishes. But as a picture of life in old China it is extremely interesting. Like all van Gulik's subsequent Magistrate Dee novels it has an authentic ring, being every bit as convincing as the original, *Dee Goong An*. This makes elaborate execution scenes, and others involving the flagellation of a lesbian woman, rather less offensive than they would have been coming from Micky Spillane or James Hadley Chase, and one takes the author's word that they come directly from the original scripts.

Elaborate torture scenes are also a recurring
feature of Japanese crime stories. The
picture (left) is from a book by Ryunsuke Akutagawa. Bottom
left: one of the many illustrations by M. Kuwata to
Edogawa Rampo's JAPANESE TALES OF MYSTERY
AND IMAGINATION, which include examples of both crime and
ghost stories. Rampo is one of Japan's most popular writers, and the
sales of his books would make even Agatha Christie green with envy.
Detective stories enjoy greater popularity in Japan than almost anywhere else, and
the number of crime magazines runs to scores. The picture (right), by
Lo Koon-Chiu, is from the cover of THE STRANGE CASES OF MAGISTRATE PAO.

The Exploits of Magistrate Pao,
which it seemed would always be
a closed book to us, was com-
mented upon at length and translated in extract by Leon Comber
with illustrations by Lo Koon-
Chiu, the publishers being
Charles E. Tuttle, Tokyo.
Entitled The Strange Cases of
Magistrate Pao, this is an un-
usually attractive and interesting
little book from which we learn
that under Chinese law a criminal
had to make a full confession
before sentence was passed.

Japan, too, is known to western connoisseurs of the detective story, for Edogawa
Rampo, her most popular mystery writer, has published some of his best short
stories in English in a collection entitled Japanese Tales of Mystery and Imagination (Tokyo, 1956). Although the genre is not nearly so old in Japan as in China,
the first detective stories, clearly bearing the marks of Chinese influence, were
written 200 years before Poe, while even before then the Japanese were reading
versions of the Pao and Dee stories. The most famous of the old Japanese crime
stories are Saikaru Ihara's Notes on Cases Heard under a Cherry Tree, which
date from 1685. But the work has never been translated, so any attempt at
evaluating the Japanese story, which has no outstanding characteristics of its
own, has to be confined to Edogawa Rampo and to two stories by Ryunsuke
Akutagawa. The classic, Chinese-influenced, stories succumbed to British and
American mystery stories, although the trail was blazed at the end of last
century by Fortune de Boisgobey and Emile Gaboriau, who enjoyed great
popularity in Ruiko Kuriowa's translations. But these are now forgotten, and
to the modern Japanese reader the name that is synonymous with the detective
story is Edogawa Rampo. The reader has only to repeat it aloud a few times to
find that he is almost saying Edgar Allan Poe – which is what the author
intended, for his real name is Hirai Taro.

Vimori Maßerina Harcourt Vimori La Procureur Harcourt Vaquary Harcourt Procureur

Maßerina Harcourt Maßerina Harcourt La Procureur Harison Maßerina Maßerina Harcourt

Maßerina Ivory Vimory piftold by Harcourt Ivory hangd and burnt Maßerina hangd Harcourt executed

The grandfather and great-grandfather of the detective story

William Godwin, the eighteenth-century English propagandist and writer, has been called 'the grandfather of the detective story'. This reputation is based on his novel of murder and the abuse of power, *Caleb Williams*.

Godwin wrote it in 1793–94 under the influence of the French Revolution. It required courage in the England of those days to attack a society under the despotic rule of landowners, in which wealth was mightier than the law.

The main character, Caleb of the title, is a detective of a kind who is spurred on by his insatiable curiosity. He flutters round the murder like a moth round a flame, with much the same contempt for his own life. Finally he is forced to flee. His account of his stretch in jail is a shocking indictment of the prison conditions of the time. He has to hide, to put on a disguise and to use all the tricks which subsequent writers so busily exploited. He sticks it out because, like Chandler's sleuth, Philip Marlow, he believes in the ultimate success of his battle for a reformed society. Godwin reveals in an appendix that, in order to ensure that his plot held the reader throughout, he built up the novel backwards.

William Godwin (1756–1836) was the first writer to exploit detective curiosity in a tautly constructed plot. Here he is seen as depicted by Daniel Maclise.

The chaplain of Newgate Prison was probably the first person to issue pamphlets containing the confessions of condemned criminals and their last words before going to the gallows. Such publications were popular reading long before the days of detectives. Left: a strip cartoon depicting a crime from start to finish in a book dramatically entitled THE TRIUMPH OF GOD'S REVENGE *(London, 1702)*. Right: the murder of a policeman as shown in THE NEWGATE CALENDAR *(1829)*.

A public execution outside Newgate Prison, London. The prison gave its name to THE NEWGATE CALENDAR, *a forerunner of the detective novel, containing stories of condemned criminals and details of how they were brought to book.*

One of the first accounts of properly organized police work appears in RECOL-LECTIONS OF A DETECTIVE POLICE OFFICER by a writer using the pseudonym of 'Waters' (1856). This frontispiece is captioned: 'The game is up, Mr Gates. I arrest you.'

The Supernatural – and a rational explanation

The tale of terror, the shocker or gothic novel, first flourished 200 years ago. It played an important role in the development of the crime novel, for many of its authors set great store by giving the apparently supernatural events they described a rational explanation, often in the form of a conversation between a clever man and a stooge. Friedrich von Schiller has a pair of the kind in his story, *Der Geistesseher*, and they might well have been the models for Sherlock Holmes and Dr Watson and many others.

The ghost in the first, and still the most famous, of all 'gothic romances', Horace Walpole's THE CASTLE OF OTRANTO *(1764). Apart from Walpole, the master in this genre is Ann Radcliffe, whose stories are set in mysterious castles with sinister counts pursuing blue-eyed heroines along murky corridors and up and down creaking spiral staircases.*

The stories of the German writer, E. T. A. Hoffmann (1776–1822), also belong to this category. FRÄULEIN SCUDERI, *for example, is set in Paris at the time of Louis XIV. The story concerns an uncanny murderer who comes and goes in silence leaving no trace behind him. Poul Christensen showed him in action for a Danish edition of the work published in 1944.*

Karen Blixen's SEVEN GOTHIC TALES *(published under her pseudonym, Isak Dinesen) is an example of modern 'gothic' writing. The above picture by the Russian artist, Majeska, is from the original American edition of* THE DELUGE AT NORDERNEY, *only 1,010 copies of which were printed, and shows a typical 'gothic' portrait gallery: a melancholy young man from Assens, a lovely young girl who has fled from a mysterious castle, a mad aristocrat, and a murderer disguised as a cardinal.*

The modern writer who more than anyone has used the supernatural in crime stories is John Dickson Carr, who also writes under the name of Carter Dickson. He calls 'the miracle problem' the most fascinating puzzle that can face a detective. His best book of the kind is *Lord of the Sorcerers*, which contains all the elements of the gothic novel, even including a ghost. But his bulky, Churchillian detective, Sir Henry Merrivale, brings everything realistically down to earth. In *The Burning Court*, however, things are less cut and dried, and it would seem as if the murderess really is a witch!

Dickens created one of the first detectives in fiction

Poe invented the first detective, and used him in three short stories. Charles Dickens created the first Anglo-Saxon detective to appear in a *novel*. This was Police-Inspector Bucket, who appears in fourteen out of the sixty-seven chapters of that absorbing work, *Bleak House*, first published in 1852-53. The fourteen chapters have also been extracted and made into a separate, self-contained book.

Bucket is a member of the London police force. A cunning old lawyer, Mr Tulkinghorn, seeks his aid to get the lovely Lady Dedlock to reveal her guilty secret. When Tulkinghorn is murdered, Lady Dedlock is suspected of the crime; so, too, is an innocent former suitor of hers. But, as in Poe's short story, *Thou Art the Man!*, the murderer proves to be the least likely person. Agatha Christie was by no means the first writer to use that device.

Bucket openly admits that his spur is the hope of a large reward. His sympathies are unhesitatingly with the strong. But he knows how to play a double game, insinuating himself into the homes of his suspects and gaining their confidence. He may be a bit ponderous but, like his successor, Maigret, he is certainly effective at clearing up problems on his own.

H. K. Browne illustrates one of the wiles of Inspector Bucket: the friendly approach. Bucket visits ex-soldier Bagnet's family on his wife's birthday. Their two girls, Quebec and Malta, sit on his knees. Behind the friendly visit there is a crafty motive: the lodger, George, leaning unsuspectingly against the mantelpiece smoking his pipe, is one of his suspects.

Left: Lady Dedlock, suspected of murder, passes a poster offering £100 reward in connection with a murder – an unpleasant reminder of her own predicament. Above: Bucket. Water-colour by Kyd (Clayton Clark).

Dickens made 'Inspector Bucket of the Detective' a true professional – one who is proud of his calling. Several of the characteristics with which he endowed him were unique at the time, though they have since become part of the stock-in-trade of the genre. Bucket was the first to assemble all the implicated, to put his cards on the table and to point to the murderer among them.

He goes through his investigations step by step, describes what they have revealed, and arrests the guilty party on the spot.

With his detective the triumphant central figure surrounded by suspects, Dickens created a model for innumerable final chapters. It is interesting, too, to see how he uses Mrs Bucket as Inspector Bucket's assistant, and has the principal suspect shadowed by her. A special chapter could be devoted to examples of married couples as detectives – and detective writers.

The Mystery of Edwin Drood
a whodunnit without the answer

In the summer of 1870, just as he had finished Chapter 23 of his crime and detective novel, *The Mystery of Edwin Drood*, Charles Dickens fell unconscious to the ground in his own dining room. He never recovered. He was fifty-eight. It was the most dramatic death in the history of the genre, for Dickens left behind what is perhaps his most fascinating work, minus an essential element – the very last thing a detective story can dispense with – the solution to the mystery. All that remains in the way of clues are one or two notes by Dickens himself and the cover drawing reproduced on the opposite page. Dickens had planned the cover in detail himself. His son-in-law, Charles Collins, brother of Wilkie Collins, drew a sketch, which Luke Fields elaborated. The interesting thing about the cover is that among the scenes depicted on it are some which appear in the concluding part of the novel and others which do not appear at all, e.g. the encounter by the light of the lamp in the cathedral crypt at the bottom, and the scene on the spiral staircase on the right. Does this cover, plus various deletions in Dickens's manuscript, give some clues to the way in which the complex intrigue in the book would have been cleared up? So many solutions to the mystery have been suggested that Mark Twain remarked: 'The investigations which a number of researchers have carried out have already thrown a great deal of darkness on the subject, and it is possible, if they continue, that we shall soon know nothing about it at all.'

The original numbers of EDWIN DROOD. *The last one was not edited by Dickens and it is possible that the sequence got changed.*

What secrets lie concealed in the crypt of Cloisterham Cathedral? How much does the drunken stonemason, Durdles, know?

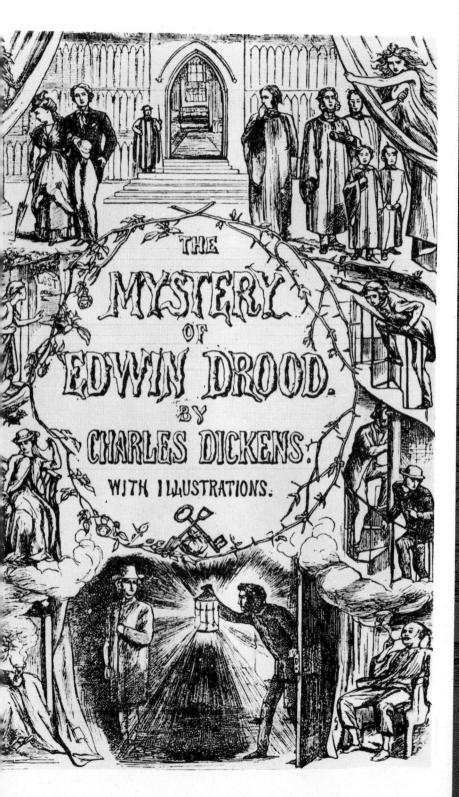

THE
MYSTERY
OF
EDWIN DROOD.
BY
CHARLES DICKENS.
WITH ILLUSTRATIONS.

Dick Datchery turns up and keeps
watch on the suspected murderer. It is
hinted that he is in disguise. The role
of the urchin 'Deputy' in the lower
drawing remains obscure.

A corpse in the cathedral crypt

Does a corpse lie hidden in the crypt of Cloisterham Cathedral? (Cloisterham is in reality Rochester, the ancient north Kent city thirty miles east of London where Dickens spent his childhood.) Is the body that of the young engineering student, Edwin Drood? Was it put into quick-lime to disintegrate in the tomb of the auctioneer and mayor, Thomas Sapsea? Is John Jasper Drood's uncle and guardian, the organist of the cathedral, the murderer? These are the questions left unanswered by Dickens's unfinished novel. A presumed murder and a presumed murderer at a fairly early stage in the book look suspicious. No doubt, as he hinted, Dickens had some unexpected cards up his sleeve to clear up the mystery. When he wrote *Edwin Drood* he was a sick man, but there is no sign of it in the book. Some of its passages are among the best he ever wrote. Professor C. A. Bodelsen, the Danish Dickens expert, has summarized the plot as follows: 'The book opens with a scene in which John Jasper is recovering from an opium stupor. John Jasper is precentor of Cloisterham Cathedral, a respected citizen whose outward conduct is wholly in keeping with the dignified atmosphere of the cathedral. People admire the solicitude with which he looks after his orphaned nephew, Edwin Drood. But in fact Jasper hates him, for Edwin is engaged to Rosa Budd, whom Jasper loves. A brother and sister, Neville and Helena Landless, come to the city from Ceylon, where they have spent their childhood. Jasper incites Neville and Edwin to quarrel, later inviting them home to a Christmas Eve dinner to make it up. The next morning Edwin has disappeared, and Neville is suspected of murdering him. Soon afterwards a man by the name of Datchery appears on the scene. There is some indication that he is in disguise, and the reader is led to believe that it is his task to solve the mystery of Edwin Drood's disappearance.' *(Dickens og hans bøger,* Copenhagen, 1957).

Let us try and reconstruct the plot by means of the following pictures.

Above: a rough draft of Jasper in the opium den, drawn by Charles Collins, Dickens's son-in-law.
Left: the stonemason, Durdles, and Jasper, the suspected murderer, in the cathedral crypt. Water-colour by Everett Shinn.

Dickens, who was a ruthless editor, even of his own work, rejected his son-in-law's sketch of Jasper in the opium den. In this illustration the atmosphere of the book's opening chapter has become even more gruesome.

Jasper (centre) incites Edwin (left) and Neville Landless, the young man from Ceylon, to quarrel, afterwards spreading the story of their altercation about the town. When Edwin disappears on Christmas night suspicion centres on Neville. This series of illustrations is by Luke Fieldes.

Jasper is madly in love with Rosa Budd. This presumably is his motive for murdering her fiancé, Edwin Drood – if murdered he was. Jasper is thought to have had hypnotic power over Rosa, as the illustration seems to suggest.

The opium woman, who is hostile to Jasper, listens to him muttering in his stupor. There is some mystery about her visit to the cathedral, where she raises her fist at him, and about her contact with the detective, Datchery. Some extraordinary theories about her include one that she is Jasper's grandmother!

Jasper faints when he hears from Rosa Budd's guardian, Grewgious, the lawyer, that her engagement to Edwin Drood has been broken off. Does he suddenly realize he has murdered in vain? The lawyer eyes him suspiciously.

Efforts to solve the mystery have included continuations of the story and essays advancing various theories. This crude picture of Edwin Drood appearing as a ghost to Jasper and Durdles, the stonemason, is from one of the many attempts to bring the book to a satisfactory conclusion.

What is the solution to the mystery of Edwin Drood?

The mystery of Edwin Drood is insoluble, says G. K. Chesterton, who acted as judge in the mock trial of John Jasper held in London in January 1914, in which well-known writers and lawyers played the roles of the characters in the book and served as jurymen. G. B. Shaw was the foreman of the jury, which found Jasper guilty. Chesterton fined Shaw and all his fellow jury members for contempt of court!

Was Edwin Drood really murdered? Or did he simply disappear – perhaps after his uncle, in an opium stupor, had tried to strangle him with his scarf? This is a theory favoured by many. But the detective, Datchery, might well be Drood in disguise returning to unmask Jasper. Could the explanation of Jasper's behaviour be that, not knowing what he did under the influence of opium, he believes himself to be a murderer? If so, then Jasper might confess to a murder he had not committed and be hanged for it – for he surely deserves to be hanged. One cannot help feeling that this is the way Dickens meant things to go. Jasper would then be a dual personality: a forerunner to Stevenson's Dr Jekyll and Mr Hyde. Once Jasper had been hanged Drood would reappear.

Most people, however, believe that Drood really was murdered. In that case, then, who is Datchery?

Datchery could, of course, simply be himself – a fresh character introduced into the story. But there is some indication that he is in disguise, and every indication that Helena Landless, an amateur actress, is clever at dis-

A scene from the mock trial of John Jasper, held in London in 1914. G. K. Chesterton, author of the Father Brown stories, is the judge. The foreman of the jury is George Bernard Shaw. Jasper was found guilty.

guises. Is she Datchery – and thus one one the world's first women detectives? Or is Datchery some other figure in the book? A case could be made out for more than one of them in the role. But no-one has succeeded in solving the mystery, for no-one can compete with the powerful imagination exerted by Dickens in the chapters he completed. There is no knowing where that imagination might have led had he lived to complete the book. Chesterton is right. Without Dickens the mystery is insoluble.

34

The Woman in White and the fat villain

Collins's second main work, ranking with The Moonstone, is The Woman in White, a harrowing story of a woman wrongfully shut up in a lunatic asylum. Complicated though the plot is it is tightly constructed. The tangled intrigue is unravelled by a newspaper artist and a brave young woman who became so popular after the publication of the story that a ship was named after her. The villains are a spurious aristocrat and a fat Italian, Count Fosco, who is a forerunner of the modern secret agent. Collins purposely made him fat and with a weakness for canaries and white mice to distinguish him from the conventional villain of the time. The 'woman in white' is an unhappy, mentally retarded girl, and the plot turns on her striking likeness to her half-sister, who is a rich heiress.

The action revolves round the fate of her fortune. Collins got the idea for the story late one night when, walking with his brother and the painter, Millais, in north London, he suddenly heard a shriek and saw a young woman dressed in white fleeing in the moonlight along what was then a country lane. Collins followed her and heard her story. She had been held a prisoner against her will. Later she became Collins's mistress. Unlike Dickens, whose secret affairs only came to light subsequently, Collins made no secret of the fact that they lived together, ignoring the disapproval of his contemporaries. Another source of inspiration to the work was a French collection of famous criminal cases which Dickens and Collins found in a second-hand bookshop in Paris.

THE WOMAN IN WHITE was dramatized with immense success. Overleaf is a reproduction of the poster that publicized the production: the first time in England that the work of a recognized artist appeared on a poster. Frederick Walker's woodcut faithfully reproduces the blend of mystery and romance in the book. The name of the artist responsible for the drawing made at the performance in 1871 (left) is unknown. Those depicted are presumably the villain, Count Fosca, and the heroine, Lady Laura.

Frederick Walker's famous poster for the stage production of THE WOMAN IN WHITE.

The detective who loved roses

Collins's novel *The Moonstone* is about the theft of a valuable and dangerous Indian jewel. The detective who clears up the crime, grey-haired Sergeant Cuff, is the first to utter the words which so many other detectives were to repeat subsequently: 'I have never known anything to be of no significance', and so he searches with relentless zeal for a piece of clothing with traces of paint on it and a laundry list. These two features were taken directly from a sensational case at the time – Constance Kent's murder of her small brother – in which they were of vital significance. Collins's detective has several characteristics in common with Inspector Whicher of Scotland Yard, who was concerned with the Kent case. But Collins gives him an additional characteristic – that of an expert on roses. Dressed in black, grey-haired and hatchet-faced (Sherlock Holmes!), he moves about the magnificently described countryside which is the scene of the crime, finally discovering the vital clue in the quicksands on the seashore.

Mysterious Indians also try to track down the moonstone, and it is they in the end who are responsible for murdering the thief. (The sinister orientals had already entered the crime genre by the time of Dickens. They have remained in it ever since.)

Opium also plays an important role in the plot. Collins was himself addicted to the drug, which he had taken to relieve the violent pains of the gout from which he suffered.

According to Collins he dictated most of the novel while under the influence of opium.

THE MOONSTONE

Left: the detective, Mr Cuff. Above: THE MOONSTONE *as a strip cartoon, with the mysterious Indians in pursuit of their sacred diamond.*

How the French began

It was no mere chance that Edgar Allan Poe made Dupin, the first detective in fiction, a Frenchman, for it was in France that the first memoirs of an ex-police detective, later a private detective, Eugene Francois Vidocq (1775–1857), were published. Vidocq began as a criminal in the stormy days of the revolution. He was constantly in and out of prison, and an expert at escape, dissimulation, forgery and disguise. Betrayed by his confederates he turned informer, and so began the second chapter of a career that carried him to the top as Chef de la Sûreté. He had little but contempt for the police he commanded. The condescending attitude towards the regular police and the general preference for the amateur, characteristic of so many crime stories, is a legacy of Vidocq, who rounded off his career as a private detective with continued success. In his memoirs he writes: 'Things had been haphazard, dependent on chance. I introduced system, and so I got results that were incomprehensible to the average person. It always astonished people reporting a theft, for example, that, given some detail which seemed insignificant to them, I could reconstruct the entire crime, or say: That man is the criminal.' Vidocq gave birth to the idea of the omniscient detective from whom nothing could be hidden.

As already mentioned, his successors in fiction were legion.

From his own experiences he had the advantage of knowing all the tricks of the underworld. And as a detective he proved a master at reconstructing a crime on the basis of a detail here, a fact there, by shadowing suspects and by following up clues. Hardly an attractive person, his strictures of the society that breeds criminals were unprejudiced and severe.

A portrait of Emile Gaboriau on the cover of the English edition of LE PETIT VIEUX DES BATIGNOLLES *(1876). Gaboriau, who was only thirty-eight when he died, was the first Frenchman to write a detective novel or 'roman-policier' and thus the founder of what has become a tradition.*

Honoré de Balzac knew Vidocq personally. His character, Vautrin, in LE PÈRE GORIOT *(Old Goriot) and other works, has some of Vidocq's characteristics. Left: Vidocq in a typically arrogant posture – an engraving from his memoirs. Right: an unknown artist's impression of Balzac's Vautrin.*

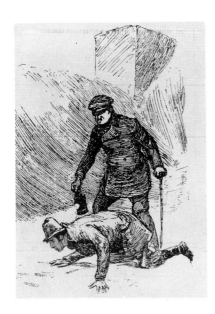

Gaboriau created several detectives, both private and official. The best known of them, police detective M. Lecoq, appears in a long series of novels. Undeterred by complexities, intrigue, and the envy of the local police, Lecoq works with arrogant self-confidence towards the solution of the mystery. The above illustration of Lecoq by Hans Nik. Hansen is from the Danish edition of a Lecoq story.

One of Balzac's novels containing a strong element of crime is *Une Ténébreuse Affaire* (The Gonderville Mystery). The work ends with a big trial scene in which the innocent are found guilty. One of the defence lawyers, a master at cross examination, makes a pronouncement which has special application in certain quarters today: 'The State is powerful for it has detectives at its disposal. The defence has not – and should have.'

Some of the earliest private detectives were solicitors chasing clues to help in their own cases. The villains in Balzac's novel were secret police agents engaged with the political rulers in a criminal conspiracy.

The big city underworld

Prince Rodolphe fighting 'the Stabber' in the shady alleys where he lived and carried on his missionary work. From LES MYSTÈRES DE PARIS.

Les Mystères de Paris is perhaps the most famous of all crime novels. Eugene Sue wrote it as a serial in 1842–43, his idea being to describe the underworld of a great city in much the same way as Fenimore Cooper had described the life of the Indians in the wilds: first the stalking of the quarry, then, in all its ferocity, the kill.

His hero, Prince Rodolphe, lives incognito in the slums, where he can help the down and out. He finds himself at odds with criminal gangs, but manages to survive much as Vidocq managed. Sue had the reforming zeal of a socialist and philanthropist, but he gave the detective genre a sense of realism. His underworld slang, for instance, is completely authentic.

Sue also wrote THE WANDERING JEW, *from which this Parisian street scene is taken. The plot involves a will, criminal conspiracies and mysterious Indians, all of them well-tried themes in the genre.*

This is probably the first edition of LES MYSTÈRES DE PARIS *in book form. Across the Seine is a view of the Île de la Cité, the haunt of criminals, symbolically situated between Notre-Dame and the Palace of Justice.*

Poking fun at the police

Twenty years after Sue, Pierre Alexis de Ponson du Terrail (1829–71) developed the crime story into something approaching the detective novel. The name of his hero, who figures in a number of stories, is Rocambole, and it is a name that can still produce a shudder.

Rocambole was the forerunner of Nick Carter and Sexton Blake, of serials full of improbable scenes and last-minute rescues.

Originally Rocambole was a street urchin, rather like 'Deputy' in Dickens's *Edwin Drood*. Later he becomes the cynical, elegant leader of his own gang.

At one point in his adventurous life he is condemned to the galleys. He manages to flee, and to avoid recognition disfigures his face with vitriol. But the public wouldn't have it – de Ponson was forced to make him recover his good looks.

As the serials continued Rocambole gradually became an adventurer-cum-private-detective, one whose greatest joy was to poke fun at the police.

He was arrogant, brave, strong in physique – a type that still flourishes in the bizarre and motley world of the detective genre.

Rocambole as the fashionably dressed leader of a criminal gang. Later, as a private detective, he continues to keep up to date, importing American revolvers of the latest type.

Rocambole in a chain gang on the long trek to the galleys at Toulon. He makes a dramatic escape, of course. The galleys haunted French fiction writers. Vidocq enjoyed the sight of the criminals he had caught being carried off to their brutal punishment. Balzac, Dumas and Hugo saw the terrible business from the galley slaves' angle.

41

Leroux and Rouletabille

While we are in France let us abandon chronology for a moment to glance at Gaston Leroux (1868–1927) and his famous detective novel *The Mystery of the Yellow Room* (Le Mystère de la chambre jaune). Many readers will have heard of the book, but few are likely to have read it. Yet it is one of the true classics. Our broad outline of the story will even reveal the murderer's identity. There is no doubt where Leroux got his inspiration from – it was from Israel Zangwill's *The Big Bow Mystery*. That gave him two things: the apparently inexplicable mystery inside the locked room, and the unexpected murderer. His detective, Joseph Rouletabille, a sixteen-year-old (!) reporter, has some of Leroux's own characteristics.

Rouletabille, the journalist playing the detective, is guided by a single principle: what common sense and observation persuade him is right.

A delightful period drawing by Simont of the pavilion used as a laboratory in the 100-year-old oak grove. The journalist and examining magistrate are on their way to interrogate Mme Stangerson, accompanied by Rouletabille's Dr Watson, an agreeable young lawyer.

LE MYSTÈRE
de la chambre jaune

PIÈCE EN CINQ ACTES
par
GASTON LEROUX

THE MYSTERY OF THE YELLOW ROOM *was of course dramatized, and the printed stage version (above) carried a photograph of Leroux. Like his hero, Leroux was a much travelled and prominent French journalist. Rouletabille inherited his author's high-handedness, and purposely gave the criminal a chance to escape.*

Journalists as detectives: there are any number of them in the genre. The most famous is E. C. Bentley's Philip Trent. Bentley was himself a journalist, though not the extrovert that Leroux was, seen below in a contemporary caricature.

Who, then, *is* the murderer in *The Mystery of the Yellow Room?* In this age of abbreviations the answer lies in the initials LSP – the least suspected person.

But Leroux carried the device one stage further, to the least suspected person of all – Police Officer Larsan, the officer engaged in solving the crime.

Since then the device has been frequently used: by Edgar Wallace, Agatha Christie, Ellery Queen, even by Raymond Chandler (in *The Lady in the Lake*). That masterly writer, Melville Davisson Post, goes even further. In his short story, *Naboth's Vineyard*, the culprit is the judge hearing the case!

43

The curious events in the yellow room

What happens in *The Mystery of the Yellow Room* is this.

A young woman scientist, Mme Stangerson, is found one evening assaulted and wounded in an hermetically sealed room in the pavilion which serves as a laboratory for her father and herself. There is no way of entering the room, which is locked on the inside. Outside the door are Mme Stangerson's father and a laboratory assistant, and when they hear her cries for help they have to break the door down in order to get in.

The case, which is investigated by Police Officer Larsan and a young journalist, M. Rouletabille, proves to be highly complex.

The investigations are carried out in the Stangersons' château and in the surrounding district, finally ending up in the criminal court at Versailles. In the château a fresh attack on Mme Stangerson occurs, and a forest ranger is murdered.

Rouletabille works through all the events muttering darkly that he knows well enough who's responsible but can't prove it.

Finally he journeys to America, where Mme Stangerson has been staying for some time, hoping to find a clue there.

In the midst of the trial he makes a dramatic return to reveal his sensational news. The arrested man is innocent. The murderer and assailant were Police Officer Larsan. Away on the other side of the Atlantic Mme Stangerson, in a state of wild infatuation, eloped with him and they got married. Soon she discovered he was a hardened criminal and fled. Larsan set after her in venomous hatred.

The attack in the yellow room had really taken place in the afternoon, but Mme Stangerson, not wanting to disclose that Larsan had attacked her, concealed her injuries. During the night, however, she cried out in her sleep, and so the attack was thought to have occurred then.

The explanation of the subsequent attacks is complicated by the fact that neither Mme Stangerson nor her new fiancé, a professor, want their secret to be revealed. The professor tacitly consents to being placed in the dock ...

The murder of the forest ranger looks highly mysterious. But it turns out that Larsan stabbed his victim from a window, appearing on the scene immediately afterwards and shouting: 'Murder! Murder!'

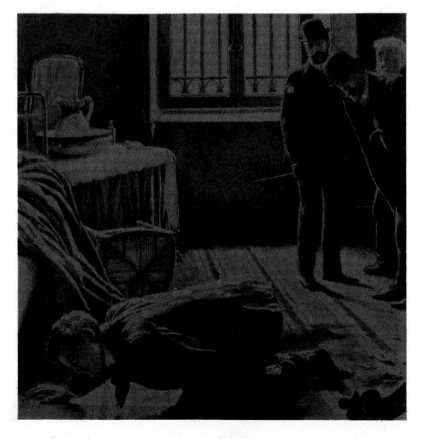

As lithe as a serpent Rouletabille slips beneath the bed. The initial examination of the locked yellow room in the pavilion cum laboratory.

Larsan has yet to be unmasked as the criminal. He stalks into the laboratory, dramatically throwing down a pair of muddy boots and saying, 'Voilà! There are the murderer's shoes. Do you recognize them?' Old Jacques, the Stangersons' servant, gapes at them.

'Mr Presiding Judge, I cannot tell you the name of the murderer before half-past-six.' Rouletabille in court, where he impudently tells the judge that he has the customary prejudices of a civil servant . . .

Arthur Conan Doyle
and
Sherlock Holmes

Sketch by D. H. Friston in the original edition of A STUDY IN SCARLET *(1887). A year later Charles Doyle, the author's father, illustrated the same book.*

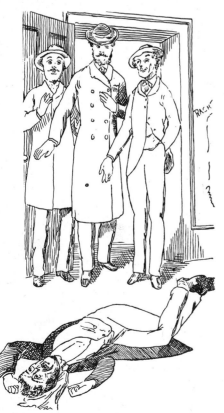

In 1887 'Beeton's Christmas Annual' contained a story by a young Scots doctor named Arthur Conan Doyle. The story, *A Study in Scarlet*, introduced a figure who was to become world famous as the greatest detective of all time – Sherlock Holmes. As a medical student Conan Doyle had had a remarkable teacher, Joseph Bell, the surgeon at the Edinburgh Infirmary, who taught at Edinburgh University Medical School. In his *Memories and Adventures*, published in 1924, Conan Doyle prints this penetrating exchange between Bell and a patient:

'Well, my man, you've served in the army?'

'Aye, sir.'

'Not long discharged?'

'No, sir.'

'A Highland regiment?'

'Aye, sir.'

'A non-com. officer?'

'Aye, sir.'

'Stationed at Barbados?'

'Aye, sir.'

'You see, gentlemen,' he would explain, 'the man was a respectful man but did not remove his hat. They do not in the army, but he would have learned civilian ways had he been long discharged. He has an air of authority and he is obviously Scottish. As to Barbados, his complaint is elephantiasis, which is West Indian and not British.'

There you have the Sherlock Holmes method in a nutshell. We need only recall the memorable moment when Dr John H. Watson was introduced to Holmes – significantly enough in a hospital – and subsequently initiated into 'the science of deduction'. Anyone interested can get the complete picture of Holmes's astonishing deductive genius by reading the episodes of Dr Watson's watch, Dr Mortimer's walking stick, Porlock's mysterious letter, and of Holmes as a thought reader. The first three are in the opening chapter of *The Sign of Four*, *The Hound of the Baskervilles* and *The Valley of Fear* respectively. The last is in *The Cardboard Box*, published in the collection entitled *His Last Bow*.

Conan Doyle's first novel caused no great stir when it was first published and brought the author a very modest fee – much less than the sum a copy of the original would now fetch – but he had plenty of time to spare at his Harley Street consulting room, where he was rarely disturbed by patients. So he could spend his time in peace and quiet thinking up ideas and making notes and drafts for the adventures of the two friends, Dr John H. Watson and Sherlock Holmes.

Arthur Conan Doyle, here seen at his desk in a sketch by Mortimer Mempes, was born in Edinburgh in 1859. He studied medicine, practising in Southsea and briefly in London before travelling to the Arctic and West Africa. He took part in the Boer War and was knighted for his patriotism. Apart from the Sherlock Holmes stories his books include a number of romances as well as works on spiritualism and criminology. He died on 7 July 1930 at his home in Windlesham.

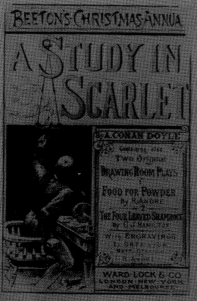

The rare first edition of A STUDY IN SCARLET, *printed in 'Beeton's Christmas Annual' for 1887. The story was published with two short stories by authors no better known than the twenty-eight-year-old doctor, who had had difficulty in finding a publisher.*

'The Strand Magazine' had the distinction of publishing the long series of Sherlock Holmes stories. The series began with *The Adventure of a Scandal in Bohemia* in the first volume of the magazine in 1891 and ended with *Shoscombe Old Place* in the March number of 1927.

Unlike the two preceding novels featuring the master detective these short stories immediately became immensely popular. People would queue up at the bookstalls to buy the latest number of 'The Strand'. And when, in 1893, Conan Doyle gave way to a fit of hatred of Sherlock Holmes and killed him off together with Professor Moriarty in the foaming waters of the Reichenbach Falls, the protests of thousands of angry readers reached such proportions that he was forced to resurrect him — an event which occurred in October 1903 in *The Empty House*. One of these same readers, an old Cornish boatman, felt nonetheless obliged to say later to Conan Doyle: 'I think, sir, when Holmes fell over that cliff, he may not have killed himself, but all the same he was never quite the same man afterwards.' The last stories are undeniably weaker in construction than the early ones. But the fact that some of the Sherlock Holmes stories are better than others, that the great detective's deductions and discoveries do not always stand up to close examination, and that chronology is sometimes hopelessly confused is of little consequence compared with the fact that Conan Doyle managed to create a pair of characters who are more alive to millions of readers than most of the world's great literary figures.

Sherlock Holmes and Dr Watson at 221B Baker Street – Victorian London

One of the charms of the Sherlock Holmes stories is the delightful atmosphere with which Conan Doyle surrounded our two friends. 221B Baker Street has never figured on any street map of London. The house the author had in mind was the then No. 21, and when, at the time of the Exhibition of Britain, 1951, Sherlock Holmes experts made part of the premises on the site into an authentic reproduction of the rooms occupied by Holmes and Watson they produced the most popular attraction outside the exhibition proper. Conan Doyle has made the bachelor quarters where so many of the Holmes stories began with a mysterious client coming to seek Holmes's help over a problem which had baffled poor Inspector Lestrade so real, that one feels one might almost join Holmes and Watson in their hansom cab as they set off on a bleak November evening with darkness falling and the gas lamps gleaming in the puddles on the shiny wet pavements.

'The Strand Magazine', which published all Conan Doyle's Sherlock Holmes short stories, from 1891 to 1927. Below: typical London exterior by an anonymous American artist illustrating THE RED-HEADED LEAGUE.

Mycroft Holmes receives a visit from his brother, Sherlock, and Dr Watson. Sherlock has come to consult Mycroft's massive intellect over the problem of THE GREEK INTERPRETER.

No-one has been more successful in conveying the peculiar atmosphere of No. 221B than
Ronald Searle (above). Right: Holmes and Watson in the Oxford Street of the nineties.
Illustration by Sidney Paget to CHARLES AUGUSTUS MILVERTON (1904).

Sidney Paget's best portrait of Sherlock Holmes: first shown to the public at an exhibition
in Abbey House, Baker Street, in 1951.

What did Sherlock Holmes look like?

Sherlock Holmes has been presented to us in a variety of guises, but in his *Memories and Adventures* Conan Doyle tells us how he himself imagined him. He saw him as very tall – over six feet – but so excessively lean that he seemed considerably taller. He had a thin razor-like face, with a great hawk's-bill of a nose, and two small eyes, set close together.

The most elegant version of Sherlock Holmes is that portrayed by the American artist, Frederic Dorr Steele. On the whole, Americans prefer Steele's illustrations to those in the typically English style by Sidney Paget, although Paget's are regarded throughout the world as the authentic ones.

The American actor, William Gillette, seen (right) in a production from 1899, was for years unrivalled in his interpretation of the master detective. The likeness to the Steele portrait is striking. Above right: the most famous screen portrayal of Holmes and Watson: Basil Rathbone and Nigel Bruce in a dramatic scene from THE HOUND OF THE BASKERVILLES, *filmed by Twentieth Century Fox in 1939.*

But Conan Doyle's picture of Sherlock Holmes changed. He writes: 'It chanced that poor Sidney Paget who, before his premature death (in 1908 at the age of forty-eight) drew all the original pictures, had a younger brother whose name, I think, was Walter, who served him as a model. The handsome Walter took the place of the more powerful but uglier Sherlock, and perhaps from the point of view of my lady readers it was as well. The stage has followed the type set up by the pictures.'

Of the many actors who impersonated Holmes on the stage Conan Doyle favoured the renowned American actor, William Gillette, of whom the brilliant American illustrator, Frederic Dorr Steele, remarked: 'There was no need to tell me that I should make *my* Sherlock Holmes look like Gillette. The thing was obvious. I always had him in my mind's eye and even copied parts of one or two stage photographs.'

Like Sidney Paget, Steele was at one with the personality of Sherlock Holmes right from the start, and among the many illustrations he drew for 'Colliers' are some of the finest portraits ever made of Holmes.

Thirty years after he had drawn the first forty-six illustrations for *The Return of Sherlock Holmes* Steele wrote that he found it curious 'that the great hawk's-bill of a nose, described in such detail (by Watson), was ignored by English artists for so many years'. But even though Steele has given Holmes a nose prominence and distinction the face is still far from that of the ugly detective first visualized by Conan Doyle, which will probably never find favour in an artist's eyes.

Unfortunately it has been impossible to find a still from the first Sherlock Holmes film, SHERLOCK HOLMES AND THE GREAT MURDER MYSTERY. A stirring drama made in 1908, the film was inspired more by Edgar Allan Poe's MURDERS IN THE RUE MORGUE than by Conan Doyle. It was 1922 before a worthy screen Holmes appeared in the person of John Barrymore with his classic profile. He had a magnificent foil in Gustave von Seyferritz as Professor Moriarty.

The illustration above, from the 1959 coloured-film version of THE HOUND OF THE BASKERVILLES, shows Holmes (Peter Cushing) and Dr Watson receiving a visit from Dr Henry Mortimer at No. 221B.

A picture from the stage production of Jerome Coopersmith's musical, BAKER STREET, with Fritz Weaver as an acceptable Holmes, Inga Swenson as a ravishing Irene Adler – the only woman in Holmes's life – and Peter Sallis as a well-nourished and sceptical Dr Watson. The music was by Marian Grudeff and Raymond Jessel, the choreography by Lee Becker Theodore.

The last dramatization of a Sherlock Holmes theme was presented on 30 October 1953 at the New Century Theatre, New York. Although Basil Rathbone played the title role, the show was a flop. And much the same fate befell Holmes in THE GREAT DETECTIVE, a ballet presented at Sadler's Wells, London, that same year. The picture shows Kenneth MacMillan as the detective.

Sherlock Holmes on the stage and screen and in ballet and operetta

The number of times different versions of the Sherlock Holmes stories have been performed in theatres all over the world is beyond computation. Hundreds have been more or less officially authorized. Sir Arthur Conan Doyle himself wrote only one play about Holmes. That was *The Speckled Band*, and it took him no more than a week to write. The world première took place at the Adelphi Theatre, London, on 4 June 1910, and two years later the work appeared in book form. The play was an enormous success. Lyn Harding as a half eliptic and wholly formidable Dr Grimsby Rylott was most masterful and stole the show from Holmes. In one respect, however, the piece was a disappointment to Conan Doyle. 'We had', he writes in his *Memories and Adventures,* 'a fine rock boa to play the title role, a snake which was the pride of my heart, so one can imagine my disgust when I saw that one critic ended his disparaging review by the words, "The crisis of the play was produced by the appearance of a palpably artificial serpent." I was inclined to offer him a goodly sum if he would undertake to go to bed with it.'

The first Sherlock Holmes play was written at the turn of the century by the famous American actor, William Gillette. He did so with Conan Doyle's blessing, playing the title role himself with great success. Once while writing another Holmes play he cabled Doyle: 'May I marry Holmes?' Doyle replied: 'You may marry or murder or do what you like with him.'

After years of triumph on the stage Holmes was transferred to the screen.

He even appeared, again with success, as the hero of a musical. That was in 1965, when Jerome Coopersmith's *Baker Street* was presented at the Broadway Theatre. The show, which was produced by Alexander H. Cohen, was given a reception by the critics similar to that accorded to *My Fair Lady* and *Around the World in Eighty Days*.

Baker Street was issued in 1966 in the 'Doubleday Theatre Series'. The plot, which is freely adapted after Conan Doyle, includes a singing Professor Moriarty – the feature which Sherlock Holmes fans probably find it most difficult to accept.

Sherlock Holmes points dramatically at the painting of wicked Sir Hugo Baskerville, the source of the curse on his family, in the Hammer Films' picture, THE HOUND OF THE BASKERVILLES, *directed by Terence Fisher (1959).*

Sherlock Holmes was kept busy even after the death of Conan Doyle. Three authors gave him the mystery of Edwin Drood to solve, Vincent Starrett confronted him with the problem of *The Unique Hamlet*, and Ellery Queen produced a pastiche called *The Misadventures of Sherlock Holmes* which had to be withdrawn when Doyle's trustees objected.

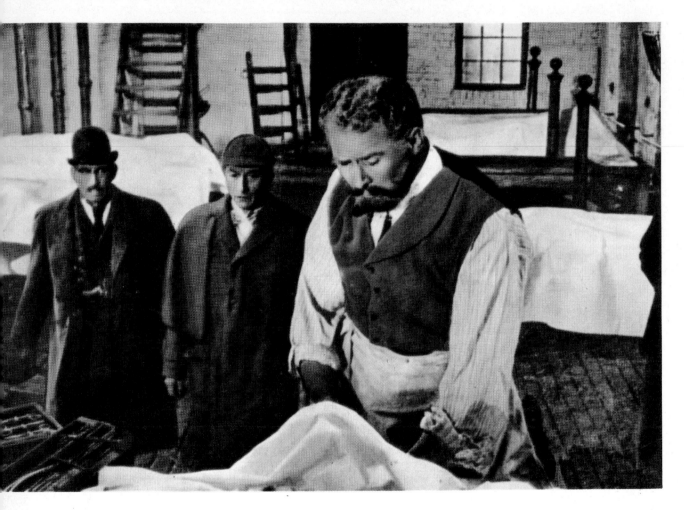

How Ellery Queen managed to get away with a veritable Sherlock Holmes novel in 1966 without encountering similar protests it is difficult to say, and few of his readers probably care. The important thing is that he managed to bring off a magnificent *tour de force* wholly in the style of the master. *A Study in Terror* starts with the detective, Ellery Queen, receiving a mysterious parcel which proves to contain some unpublished notes by Dr John H. Watson. These reveal a fascinating story of how Sherlock Holmes discovered, and helped to put out of harm's way, the bestial mass murderer, Jack the Ripper, who struck fear into the hearts of Londoners in the autumn of 1888 and caused a sensation throughout the civilized world by murdering six drunken prostitutes in the slums of London's East End. The crimes appeared to be motiveless, and when the murderer disappeared with as little trace as when he had come the most fantastic theories were advanced regarding his identity. On one point, however, most of the theories agreed: the murderer had received medical training and was a man of culture.

Two colour stills from the film A STUDY IN TERROR. *Above: Watson (Donald Houston) and Holmes (John Neville) visit Dr Murray, who is examining the body of one of the murdered women. Right: Holmes and Watson in evening dress are attacked by a pair of roughs after investigating 'The Angel and Crown', a shady pub where Angela, her face disfigured, is concealed from the world in the flat of the dubious Max Steiner above the bar.*

Sherlock Holmes
solves the mystery of Jack the Ripper

The idea of setting Sherlock Holmes to solve the mystery of Jack the Ripper was brilliant, and Ellery Queen's treatment of it is masterly. Ellery had to find the sender of the anonymous manuscript and demonstrate that for once Dr Watson (though not, of course, Sherlock Holmes) had been wrong. The American section of the novel is in Ellery Queen's own style, while Dr Watson's notes are in the authentic Victorian idiom, thus increasing the illusion. Ellery Queen's knowledge of both the fictional Sherlock Holmes and the all too real Jack the Ripper is exhaustive.

It might be objected that such a horrifying episode in crime history as the mystery of Jack the Ripper is hardly a fitting subject for light reading, and there is no denying that the author had to cope with some terrible scenes.

But this did not prevent Herman Cohen from producing a colour film of the book which, under the direction of James Hill, was hardly less bloody. Hill dropped Ellery Queen's part and concentrated on Sherlock Holmes and Jack the Ripper. But the denouement was the same as Queen's, and the film gave a realistic impression of London by gaslight. The part of Holmes was played by John Neville, the controversial former artistic director of Nottingham Playhouse and a worthy successor in a most exacting role to John Barrymore, Clive Brook and Basil Rathbone.

The Hound of the Baskervilles

Above: the first edition of THE HOUND OF THE BASKERVILLES, *published in London in 1902 by George Newnes. It contained sixteen of the sixty illustrations drawn by Sidney Paget for 'The Strand Magazine', in which the story originally appeared. Paget also designed the attractive cloth binding. Below: Valdemar Andersen designed the binding and dust jacket for the first Danish edition of* THE ADVENTURES OF SHERLOCK HOLMES, I–IX, *(1893–1902).*

The Hound of the Baskervilles has often been acclaimed as the best detective story ever written.

When the book first began to appear as a serial in 'The Strand Magazine' in August 1901 Sherlock Holmes had been 'dead' for more than seven years, and the world had mourned and pilgrimaged to the foot of the Swiss mountain beneath the Reisenbach Falls where the mortal remains of Holmes were said to lie. While visiting his friend, Fletcher Robinson, Conan Doyle heard him recount a West Country legend which had originally been told to Max Pemberton. It was to this that the tale owed its inception. *The Hound of the Baskervilles* had already become a classic by the time it appeared in book form. Christopher Morley writes of it: 'From the moment when Holmes, looking at Mrs Hudson's well-polished silver coffee pot sees the image of Watson studying the "Penang lawyer" (a walking stick) the reader is carried in an absorption we would not spoil by giving any hints. Holmes rarely laughed and when he did so it bodied ill for evildoers. Towards the end of this superb tale we hear his strident and dangerous mirth.'

The delightful atmosphere of these stories has been evoked by Robert Storm Petersen, the great Danish humorist: 'And now let me take Conan Doyle down from the shelf. The heavy winter curtains are drawn across the window – I settle down into a big armchair, my legs up on another, three different tins of tobacco on the table beside me, two or three pipes – the black clay one filled with Gallaher's "Iron King" – a stiff whisky and soda – and I'm ready for Sherlock Holmes. 'The fire crackles in the grate, send-ing a soft red glow across the carpet – the clock on the mantelpiece ticks away and gently strikes the hour – outside the autumn wind sighs in the tall poplars – the smoke from my pipe settles in a low blue cloud over the room – and I'm off with Holmes and Watson across the heath in search of a clue that will reveal the whereabouts of the bicycle-riding teacher from the Priory School. . . . Was that a noise behind the curtain over there? Is it Holmes and Watson breathlessly waiting in Charles August Milverton's comfortable room while noting the smell of his fine Havana cigar?

'Or are we out on the foggy heath in *The Hound of the Baskervilles* – or in the lonely house in *A Study in Scarlet*? Wherever it is the atmosphere of these remarkable and ever delightful stories has me in its grip.

'I hear the nightwatchman's steps out on the gravel in the garden, I lift the curtain and watch the big clouds moving like vultures across the silver face of the moon.

'I fill a pipe with "Honey Dew", wind up the musical box, and with its tinkling notes sounding in the distant darkness turn to just one more story: *The Man with the Twisted Lip*.'

It is the details that matter to Sherlock Holmes – just as they do to his readers. Consider this exchange from *Silver Blaze*:

Inspector Gregory: Is there any point to which you would wish to draw my attention?

Holmes: To the curious incident of the dog in the night-time.

Inspector Gregory: The dog did nothing in the night-time.

Holmes: That was the curious incident.

CONAN DOYLE:

A SCANDAL IN BOHEMIA

Conan Doyle's famous short story starts with the visit of a masked and disguised figure to Holmes's rooms in Baker Street. The visitor proves to be King Wilhelm of Bohemia! Irene Adler, the American prima donna, is threatening to compromise him . . .

An American comic strip version of the first Sherlock Holmes short story, A SCANDAL IN BOHEMIA. More faithful to the original than most, it was the work of two American artists, Edith Meisner and Frank Giacoia, and appeared in 1954.

The whole Sherlock Holmes and Dr John H. Watson saga consists of four novels: *A Study in Scarlet* (1877), *The Sign of Four* (1890), *The Hound of the Baskervilles* (1902), and *The Valley of Fear* (1915), together with fifty-six short stories published between 1891 and 1927 – not a vast production, but enough to secure the author a niche in world literature and – something that is rare – a lasting place in the hearts of his readers.

The terror novel

Purists refuse to have terror novels in their collection of crime books – mistakenly, in our view, for many of them are crime stories in the original sense of the term, and without them the overall picture and history of the genre would be incomplete. We would include without hesitation H. G Wells's 'grotesque romance' *The Invisible Man* (1897). R. L. Stevenson's *The Strange Case of Dr Jekyll and Mr Hyde* is dealt with at some length later in this book. For the moment let us glance at two of the more famous gothic novels. Bram Stoker's *Dracula* appeared in 1897 and became an immediate success. The author, who was born in Dublin in 1847, died in 1912 of overstrain, so did not live to see the further success of his work on the stage and screen. He started life as a clerk, became a dramatic critic, an editor, produced cheap fiction, and then came into contact with the great Shakespearian actor, Henry Irving. Stoker became manager of the Lyceum Theatre, London, for Irving, where the great actor performed with Ellen Terry as his leading lady, and this was the introduction to a lifelong friendship between the three – a friendship which stood up to the test when in 1898 Irving suffered great financial losses and damage to his health. Stoker worked hard to set the Lyceum on its feet again although *Dracula* had come out a few months earlier and was earning him good money.

Stoker got the idea of the vampire in *Dracula* from Sheridan Le Fanu's *Carmilla*. But Stoker's novel was to be quite different, and after lengthy research he found a model in Dracole Waida, who ruled Wallachia from 1456 to 1464.

*William Fitzgerald's sinister castle in
Bram Stoker's* UNDER THE SUNSET *became
even more uncanny as Dracula's home
in the Carpathians sixteen years later.*

DOCTOR·NIKOLA

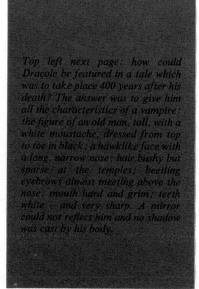

*Top left next page: how could
Dracole be featured in a tale which
was to take place 400 years after his
death? The answer was to give him
all the characteristics of a vampire:
the figure of an old man, tall, with a
white moustache, dressed from top
to toe in black; a hawklike face with
a long, narrow nose; hair bushy but
sparse at the temples; beetling
eyebrows almost meeting above the
nose; mouth hard and grim; teeth
white — and very sharp. A mirror
could not reflect him and no shadow
was cast by his body.*

Sinister Chinamen, secret societies, strange exotic lands, horrible dwarfs, a black cat, and one of the queerest master minds in fiction fascinated readers by the hundred thousand when Guy Boothby's *Doctor Nikola* first appeared in serial form in 'The Windsor Magazine' in 1896. The series of books that followed made Boothby one of the most widely read English writers of the day. Curiously enough, Dr Nikola's adventures were never apparently filmed, although in the early days of Danish films Robert Storm Petersen seriously considered doing them. He writes: 'The film called for a number of Chinese dwarfs. We did have one dwarf, and a genuine Chinese one at that, and the whole film really revolved round him. The idea was to take shots of him in all imaginable situations, to give the impression of a whole crowd of dwarfs. But the film never came to anything. Difficulties over a clifftop castle with a boiling sea in the background, a night in Venice, wolves chasing Nikola across barren steppes, and many other expensive scenes made it impossible.'

Picturesque
master criminals

Tales of romantic robbers are centuries older than detective stories. Robin Hood of Sherwood Forest, who robbed from the rich to give to the poor, is known all over the world. There was a similar myth in eighteenth-century England about Dick Turpin, a common cattle thief and murderer who was romanticized into a noble highwayman. Italian bandits were glorified in much the same way, a fact which gave K. and Hesketh Prichard the idea for two collections of short stories, THE CHRONICLES OF DON Q (1904–6). Below: Don Q, drawn by Stanley L. Wood.

The earliest work on criminals is a little volume published by Peter Wagner in Nuremberg in about 1488. Entitled *Dracole* it was a real shocker, describing the frightful misdeeds of Dracole Waida from 1456 to 1464. The book contains the oldest known portrait of a famous criminal: a crude, hand-coloured woodcut showing a grim-faced Dracole with long black hair and a heavy moustache, crowned with an elegantly fashioned high-crowned hat embellished with a large jewel. Next came Shakespeare's murderers – unsurpassed in fact or fiction. But to the devotee of crime literature the stars of the rogues' gallery are Professor James Moriarty and his friend, 'the second most dangerous man in London', Colonel Sebastian Moran. It was Professor Moriarty who nearly sent Holmes to his death in their mortal struggle at the Reichenbach Falls. But Holmes had to admit to Watson on returning from his exploration of Tibet: 'From the point of view of the criminal expert, London has become a singularly uninteresting city since the death of the late lamented Professor Moriarty.' In *The Final Problem* Holmes describes Moriarty as follows: 'He is the Napoleon of crime. He is the organizer of half that is evil and of nearly all that is undetected in this great city. He is a genius, a philosopher, an abstract thinker. He has a brain of the first order. He sits motionless, like a spider in the centre of its web, but that web has a thousand radiations, and he knows well every quiver of each of them. . . . This was the organization which I deduced, Watson, and which I devoted my whole energy to exposing and breaking up.' Holmes succeeded only in part. Moriarty was disposed of, but in *The Empty House* Holmes realizes that Colonel Sebastian Moran, second-in-command of the organization, is still very much alive. Holmes has to get back to work – this time against a man with the career of an honourable soldier behind him who, now that Moriarty is dead, is the most cunning and dangerous criminal in London.

Soon after the war Sir Alexander Korda commissioned Graham Greene to write a film set against the four-power occupation of Vienna. The result was THE THIRD MAN, a film in which Orson Welles as Harry Lime created one of the most realistic screen villains of our time. Opposite page: Harry Lime in a thrilling scene in the sewers of Vienna. In 1950 Graham Greene made the screen-play into a novel, which was published with the book of another successful film of his, THE FALLEN IDOL. ▶

Sapper's Hugh ('Bulldog') Drummond had a worthy adversary in Carl Peterson, who had many of the characteristics of Professor Moriarty – though not the Professor's coolness towards women. Below: Nigel Green as the master criminal in a recent film. After a trial of strength with Drummond, Peterson is brought down by a mechanical chess player which has been his pride and joy.

Professor Moriarty as portrayed by Sidney Paget for THE FINAL PROBLEM. *'He is extremely tall and thin,' says Holmes, 'his forehead domes out in a white curve, and his two eyes are deeply sunken in his head.'*

The curiosity
of detectives

To see and observe, to be curious and alert, to draw conclusions from what one sees – the art was known to fiction long before Poe created Dupin and wrote of the philosophy of deduction.

In 1719 a nobleman by the name of Mailly published in Paris: *The Voyages and Adventures of the Three Princes of Serendip, translated from the Persian.* It is not true, however, that it came from Persia. The fable has many sources and parallels, and testifies to the existence of a long-standing interest in the art of detection. It runs like this. Three princes are asked: 'Have you seen a stray camel?' They reply: 'No, but we can describe it.' And they describe it so accurately that they are accused of stealing it and are brought before the emperor. The emperor asks them: 'If you are innocent, how ever can you know that the camel is blind in one eye, is lame, and has lost a tooth?' They reply: 'The camel had eaten grass on one side of the road only, although there was plenty of grass on the other. It had left tufts of partly chewed grass the size of a tooth. And its tracks clearly showed that it dragged one foot.'

This tale gave the English language the word 'serendipity', signifying the faculty of making happy discoveries by accident, which these princes possessed.

The magnifying glass – part of the classic equipment of the detective. Even Maigret used one in his youth. (Early Simenon betrays the influences of Croft.) The picture shows Sherlock Holmes with one in THE NORWOOD BUILDER.

'Hark! What's that?' The detective on the alert, with his companion – and chronicler of his adventures – in the background. Painting by Gayle Hoskins for THE STRANGE CASES OF MASON BRANT *(1916),, by Neville Monroe Hopkins.*

Above: disguise, the classic device of the investigator. The Italian priest is Sherlock Holmes in disguise in THE FINAL PROBLEM *(illustration by Sidney Paget). Oddly enough, Holmes disguised himself as a clergyman in Doyle's very first short story about him,* A SCANDAL IN BOHEMIA. *Below: the sign of Stuart Palmer is a reminder that detectives can also be women. Palmer invented the zealous amateur who is something of a tease in the person of Miss Hildegarde Withers, in private life a teacher. But more of women later.*

Another classic example of popular interest in observation and deduction is Voltaire's philosophical story of the unfortunate young man, Zadig (1747).

Zadig is accused of stealing the queen's dog and the king's horse. But the reason he knows so much about them is that he has observed their tracks. The dog, says Zadig, is a bitch, and very small and shaggy. It has recently whelped, is lame in the left fore-paw and has extremely long ears.

From its tracks Zadig noticed that its teats trailed in the sand, so it must have been female, short in the leg and have whelped recently. Its long ears also left trail marks, while its paw marks clearly indicated a limp. And even if the teat marks had not suggested the creature's height, that could be deduced from traces where it had passed through a thicket.

A number of writers, including both Balzac and Poe, refer to Zadig, who is one of the original omniscient detectives – the kind who rouse astonishment in all around them merely by practising the art of using their eyes.

The height of superiority in such a detective is achieved in *The House of the Arrow* (A. E. W. Mason) where the sleuth boasts: 'Of course I see something. Always I see something. Am I not Hanaud?... the Hanauds must see something everywhere – even when there is nothing to see.'

Gaboriau the pioneer

We have already mentioned the French writer, Emile Gaboriau, and his detectives. Gaboriau was the first to lay the emphasis throughout his novel on the work of detection rather than on the criminal and the crime. He was also the first writer of detective stories to achieve worldwide success, although Conan Doyle with Sherlock Holmes eventually surpassed him. Gaboriau admired Poe and gave his principal detective, M. Lecoq, similar qualities to those possessed by M. Dupin: the ability to see, to analyse, and to produce results that astonished his companions. Conan Doyle was impressed by the work of Gaboriau. The inventive young Frenchman always laid a false trail and provided a denouement based on a trick. He was the first to illustrate his text with a sketchmap of the scene of the crime. He was also the first with a sleuth who makes plaster casts of footprints. Gaboriau has earned a niche in the history of the detective story.

The riding boot that left the footprint: Margaret Rutherford on the job as Agatha Christie's Miss Marple in the film version of MURDER AT THE GALLOP *(MGM).*

A photographer is the most obvious of all observers. Below: James Stewart peers through his camera straight into the world of murder. From the Hitchcock film, REAR WINDOW *(Paramount).*

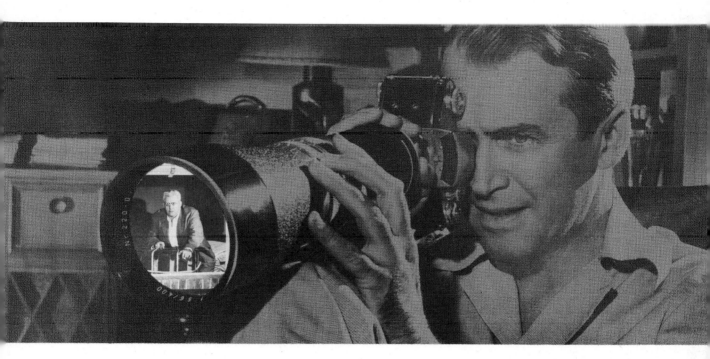

The villain unmasked. But Colonel Clay, the man tearing off the disguise, is himself an early example of a gentleman crook. Drawing by Gordon Browne for Grant Allen's AN AFRICAN MILLIONAIRE *(1897).*

Theses could be written on the astuteness of detectives and the inventiveness of their authors. Learned papers could be devoted to the use of disguise, to such things as finger-prints, magnifying glasses, revolvers, the art of shadowing, means of transport and methods of interrogation.

Why are dogs so seldom used in the genre? They play an important role in police work in real life. Part of the reason for the lapse is, we believe, that the curiosity and the reasoning capacity of man are far more interesting than the instinct of a dog. A strong story told by a clever, professional 'eavesdropper' has something satisfying about it. To the detective no doors are closed. There is nothing he cannot get to the bottom of. With him we go behind the scenes of the most secret and complex cases and have everything explained.

There is something very gratifying in all this and it is, perhaps, the main reason for the abiding fascination of detectives all over the world.

Then again there is the relaxation of watching other people at work – and detectives are usually extremely energetic people, rushing hither and thither, tirelessly collecting one piece of the jigsaw puzzle after another and fitting them together for us. Gaboriau's Lecoq has only to look at the snow-covered ground outside an inn to describe immediately the man who passed by half an hour earlier. He is middle-aged, very tall, wears a shaggy overcoat and is married!

65

The Mystery of a Hansom Cab

The detective story that headed the list of British best sellers in the last century was written neither by Wilkie Collins nor by Conan Doyle. Entitled *The Mystery of a Hansom Cab* it was the first novel by an Anglo-Australian writer, Fergus W. Hume. It first appeared in Melbourne in 1887 and was published later the same year in London by a firm that clearly had nothing to learn about marketing a commodity. The mother country was in any case a ready market, for interest in Australia ran high, while the public of those days was not nearly so exacting in the way of logically constructed plots as readers of today, nurtured as they are on a diet of sophisticated crime writing. All the same, it seems incredible that over half a million copies of what now seems such a tedious book could have been sold by the time of the author's death. It is a mystery how hundreds of thousands of copies of such a shocker could be devoured by enthusiastic readers so that even the British Museum, which normally has a copy of all original editions, has to be content with a specimen of the 225th thousand. The answer probably lies in the curious system of numbering adopted by the publishers, the phrase '. . . th thousand' on the title page being no more than a trick to advertise the book.

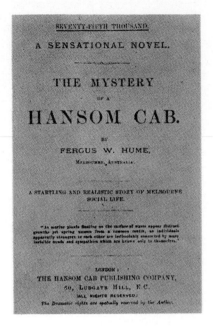

Fergus W. Hume was born in England in 1859, though he spent three years of his childhood in Dunedin, New Zealand, and three years of his youth in Melbourne before returning in 1888 to the island of his birth. By the time of his death from a cerebral affection at his home in Essex in 1932 he had managed to publish no less than 136 crime novels, all of which leaned heavily on the reputation of *The Mystery of a Hansom Cab*. None of them surpasses his first work – which, from the literary point of view, is not saying much. But there is one achievement Fergus W. Hume does have to his credit : the popularization of the delightful hansom cab among his contemporaries in crime writing. The hansom cab was a means of transport often used by Holmes and Watson, while Frank Heller, the Swedish writer, in his entertaining short stories about the gentlemen crook, Filip Collin, kept it going right up to the time of the First World War. Despite his fondness for the hansom cab, Filip Collin first appeared in a book about a car, *Automobilen 12 M 1000*, but never took to the air.

Veteran cars have a charm of their own. And at the turn of the century, when they were new, they were a sign of wealth and dash. This remarkable vehicle with its fur-clad driver and hero and heroine, painted by Rasmus Christiansen in 1909, graces the cover of one of the earliest Danish detective stories, by a writer using the pseudonym of Niels Vivild.

The aircraft depicted below is also a veteran and is described by Graham Greene in THE SPY'S BEDSIDE BOOK as 'the new British Army Aeroplane'. Rough sketch, drawn by Lt Karl Strauss of the German Secret Service.

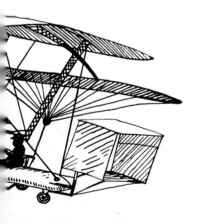

Some picturesque hansom cabs by Yngve Berg (1914), S. G. Hulme Beaman (1930), and Bertil Lybeck (1916). The photograph shows a London hansom cab outside Greenwich station in the eighties.

The most famous of
all terror stories

Left: Dr Jekyll, the respected citizen, becomes transformed in his laboratory into the monster, Hyde. Illustration by S. G. Hulme Beaman. Below: William Brodie, by day a prominent councillor and business man, by night a thief – a character inspired by Stevenson's work.

R. L. Stevenson, author of *Treasure Island*, never wrote a crime or detective story as such. But crime and its solution frequently figured in his plots, and he was responsible for the most famous horror story of all, a literary masterpiece on the mixture of good and evil in man's nature: *The Strange Case of Dr Jekyll and Mr Hyde*. A London lawyer, Mr Utterson, acting as a kind of detective, gradually discovers that Dr Jekyll, a respected physician, can change himself by means of a drug he has discovered into a personality that absorbs all his evil instincts. This personality becomes the monster and murderer, Mr Hyde.

This short novel embodies powerful drama and terrifying symbolism.

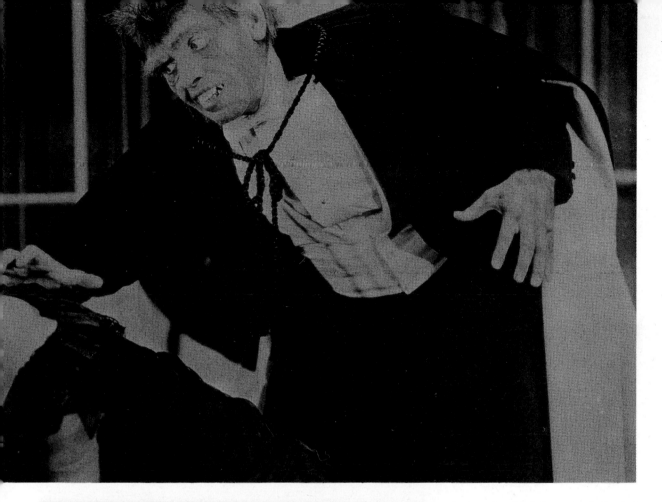

Stevenson's tale of the man with the dual personality has been filmed several times. The title role makes heavy demands on the actor and make-up artist, while the ingenuity of the technicians enables the transformation to take place before our eyes. The scene above shows Frederic March and Miriam Hopkins in Rouben Mamoulian's film of 1931 (Paramount).

The most famous of all Mr Hydes was John Barrymore in 1919, also by Paramount.

The pervasive gloom of the London fog

An innocent pedestrian is murdered by Hyde. An impression by Paul Høyrup.

Jean Louis Barrault in Jean Renoir's Gallicized version of Stevenson's DR CORDELIER'S TESTAMENT.

Dr Jekyll and Mr Hyde is redolent of London, and the book is one of many to have inspired Conan Doyle. Consider these lines on the London fog: 'It was by this time about nine in the morning, and the first fog of the season. A great chocolate-coloured pall lowered over heaven, but the wind was continually charging and routing these embattled vapours; so that as the cab crawled from street to street, Mr Utterson beheld a marvellous number of degrees and hues of twilight; for here it would be dark like the back-end of evening; and there would be a glow of a rich, lurid brown, like the light of some strange conflagration; and here, for a moment, the fog would be quite broken up, and a haggard shaft of daylight would glance in between the swirling wreaths. The dismal quarter of Soho seen under these changing glimpses, with its muddy ways, and slatternly passengers, and its lamps, which had never been extinguished or had been kindled afresh to combat this mournful re-invasion of darkness, seemed, in the lawyer's eyes, like a district of some city nightmare.'

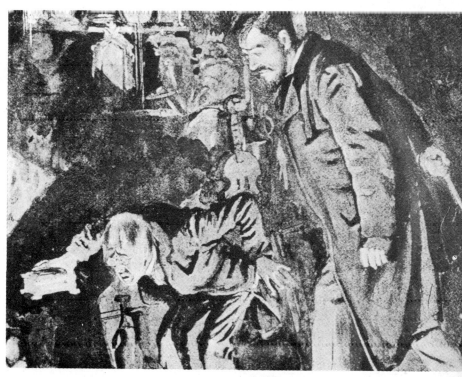

It is Christmas Day. Children are singing carols in the house next door. In the antique shop Markheim murders the old proprietor. Afterwards he talks to the personification of his own conscience – another variant of the dual personality motif. The murder in Stevenson's famous thriller, MARKHEIM, *as depicted by Harold Copping.*

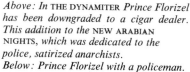

Above: In THE DYNAMITER *Prince Florizel has been downgraded to a cigar dealer. This addition to the* NEW ARABIAN NIGHTS, *which was dedicated to the police, satirized anarchists.*
Below: Prince Florizel with a policeman.

In Stevenson's *New Arabian Nights*, Prince Florizel of Bohemia roams through London like Prince Rudolph in Sue's *Les Mystères de Paris*. The prince is bored and longs for adventure. A young man he meets in a bar takes him to a suicide club where each night the members play a deadly game of poker. The player who is dealt the ace of spades has to be murdered – by the player who is dealt the ace of clubs. The prince is dealt the ace of spades. Such is the introduction to a number of imaginative and elegant tales about a naive young American in Paris, of the intrigue surrounding a corpse which has to be got rid of, and of the search for the villainous president of the suicide club, a super-criminal in the manner of Balzac's Ferragus. In the course of a duel the prince kills him. Other crime stories reveal Stevenson in all his charm. A favourite of ours is *The Pavilion on the Links*, a story set on the Scottish shore of the 'German Ocean' involving a dilapidated mansion-house and a small pavilion or belviedere in which are gathered in curious circumstances a young aristocrat, a rascally banker, a beautiful young girl, and a group of mysterious Italians. Camping outside in the sand hills on the links is the narrator, one of those open-air Englishmen who is happiest when sleeping out of doors in the wind and rain with a blanket and fire. An inexplicable nocturnal landing on the deserted coast, a light suddenly appearing in the empty pavilion, a manhunt in the otherwise law-abiding countryside, fog and quicksands all combine to make a masterly story. Stevenson raises crime fiction to the level of art.

'Lady detectives'

Exactly twenty years after the publication of the first detective story the world's first woman detective, Mrs Paschal, made her début in a collection of short stories, *The Experiences of a Lady Detective*, published anonymously in London in 1861. Mrs Paschal relates how, suddenly finding herself devoid of means on the death of her husband, she was offered a job that was remarkable, exciting and mysterious. She accepted without hesitation and became 'one of those much feared but little known persons called lady detectives', doing so, moreover, at the age of forty or thereabouts. Mrs Paschal's brain, as she herself says in all modesty, was well developed, she came of good family and had had an excellent education, so that given her skill as an actress she was able to take on any case with confidence, acumen, and unlimited means. After all this, one might imagine that she would prove to be one of the great scientific detectives; in fact her 'experiences' are slightly tedious. More to our taste are the younger and rather more attractive ladies who succeeded her: Catherine Louise Parkis's *Loveday Brooke* (1894) from the detective bureau in Lynch Court, Grant Allen's something of a blue-stocking, Lois Cayley, in *Miss Cayley's Adventures* (1899), or M. McDonnell Bodkin's *Dora Myrl* (1900) who, nine years after her début, marries the author's male detective, Paul Beck.

Baroness Emmuska Orczy was one of the first new twentieth-century writers in the detective field. Born in 1865 in Hungary she went as a young girl to London to study art, marrying the painter, Montagu Barstow. Her earliest detective stories appeared in 'The Royal Magazine' in 1901. Nine years later she launched one of the most thrilling of official women detectives, delightful Lady Molly, who was given the opportunity of exercising her skill and charm in only that one collection of stories, LADY MOLLY OF SCOTLAND YARD.

Frontispiece by an unknown American artist to Katharine Green's THE HOUSE IN THE MIST (1905)

Lady Molly of Scotland Yard has the situation under control. Illustration by Cyrus Cuneo, 1910.

Mary Roberts Rinehart's most famous crime story, THE CIRCULAR STAIRCASE, was published in New York in 1908. Three of her women sleuths were Lititia Carberry, Louise Baring and Nurse Hilda Adams.

The most famous woman detective of all is Agatha Christie's ingenious spinster, Miss Jane Marple, of whom more later. Meanwhile, to continue with other well-known women in the genre: Anna Katharine Green had the honour of carrying on the Poe tradition in the US. Her first novel, *The Leavenworth Case*, appeared in 1878. In addition to being the first detective novel written by an American it is an excellent book, as much pleasure to read now as when it was published nearly a hundred years ago. Katharine Green's only 'lady detective', Violet Strange, appears in a collection of short stories entitled *The Golden Slipper* (1915). Other women detectives featured in books are, in chronological order: George R. Sims's *Dorcas Deene*; Fergus W. Hume's *Hagar Stanley*; Arthur B. Reeve's *Constance Dunlap*; Hubert Footner's *Madame Rosika Storey*; Agatha Christie's *Tup-* pence Beresford; F. Tennyson Jesse's *Solange Fontaine*; Mignon G. Eberhart's *Susan Dare*; Frances and Richard Lockridge's *Mrs North*; G. D. H. and M. Cole's *Mrs Warrender*; A. A. Fair's *Bertha Cool*; Stuart Palmer's *Hildegarde Withers* and Hugh Travers's *Madame Aubry*.

Loveday Brooke in a trap. Sketch by Bernard Higham.

Damsels in distress

Cover drawing by Kaj Olsen for THE ANGELIC AVENGERS *by Pierre Andrezel (Karen Blixen), a pastiche of French serials featuring 'ladies in distress'.*

The damsel-in-distress motif naturally occurs in many parodies of the genre. The dark deed portrayed below was drawn by Luxius Hitchcock for Mark Twain's satirical tale, A DOUBLE BARRELLED DETECTIVE STORY *(1902).*

'Damsel in distress' is a popular theme in the crime genre and one going back to the gothic novel. With its emphasis on sympathy for the women involved the theme has always been a difficult one to link with the activities of the thoroughly logical detective. Masculine critics have dubbed it HIBK – 'Had I But Known'. 'Had I but known what I now know I could have . . .' The damsel fails to tell the police what she knows and so finds herself facing fresh perils. Mary Roberts Rinehart, author of *The Circular Staircase*, is reputed to have created the form. But there are several such scenes in, for example, Mignon G. Eberhart's stories. The nurse in her novel, *The Patient in Room 18* (1929), can never get hold of her eccentric sleuth (with servant) when the thought of doing so finally occurs to her. And when she does try it is too late. The electric light goes out again and once more there is a murder. . . . The best HIBK novel is Mabel Seeley's witty story, *The Listening House*.

Above: the murderer climbs up the sheet intended for the girl's lover (Japanese story). Right: Madeleine Carroll in peril in Hitchcock's film of the Somerset Maugham spy story, ASHENDEN. Below: pastoral scene from an English almanac.

Curious types

Ellis Parker Butler introduced a novel type of sleuth in 1918 with his PHILO GUBB, CORRE-SPONDENCE-SCHOOL DETECTIVE.

'Crime', says The Old Man in the Corner to Miss Mary Burton, the journalist who acts as his 'Watson', 'only interests me when it is a complex game of chess full of crafty moves,' introducing himself as the first 'armchair detective'. Drawing by H. M. Brock.

After Sherlock Holmes there was no limit to the queerness and eccentricity of detectives. In three collections of short stories (1914–27), Ernest Bramah created a blind master detective, Max Carrados, with great tact and sensitivity. Professor Augustus S. F. X. van Dusen, Ph.D., LL.D., F.R.S., M.D. and M.D.S., the monstrous cerebral man, appeared almost by chance in the final chapters of *The Chase of the Golden Plate* (1906) by the American writer, Jacques Futrelle, and then became the chief character in *The Thinking Machine* and in two collections of short stories.

Baroness Orczy's *The Old Man in the Corner* (1901) introduced the anonymous old gentleman in the check ulster with the big horn-rimmed spectacles, rasping voice, runny nose and thin bony fingers, constantly playing with a piece of string as he sat at his regular table in a London ABC teashop, a glass of milk or cup of coffee in front of him, solving the most complicated crimes solely by logical thinking and never bothering to go to the scene of the crime or utilize any aid but a few brief newspaper reports. *The Old Man in the Corner*, containing the first twelve short stories, appeared in book form in 1909 – curiously enough four years *after* the rather weaker companion book, *The Case of Miss Elliot*. The third volume, *Unravelled Knots*, was published as recently as 1926. Baroness Orczy's two other detective oddities are Napoleon's police spy, M. Fernand, chief character in *The Man in Grey* (1918), and Patrick Mulligan, a brilliant lawyer, who appears in a collection of short stories, *Skin o' My Tooth* (1925).

Incidentally, both Baroness Orczy and Ellery Queen regard the Scarlet Pimpernel as one of the great detectives.

'The Thinking Machine', from the most famous of Jacques Futrelle's short stories, THE PROBLEM OF CELL 13. *After a bet he manages to escape from the condemned cell in the Chrisholm Prison. Drawing by C. Beck.*

The only detective in the tradition of J. Fenimore Cooper's Red Indian pathfinders is Hesketh Prichard's *November Joe* (1911), whose adventures are also set in the great forests and who can be seen following a trail above right. As fur trapper, scout and guide he has all the qualifications for tracking down criminals in the vast expanses of Canada, where he is often the sole custodian of the law for hundreds of miles around. As Sir Andrew says, if you had committed a murder he would be the very last person you would want to have on your tracks.

The hero of Gelett Burgess's *The Master of Mystery*, published a year after *November Joe,* is a very different type of character. The book is cunningly contrived to contain two code messages. Although it was published anonymously, the initial letter of the first word of each of the twenty-four stories spells out: 'The author is Gelett Burgess'. Similarly, the last letter of the last word of each story spells out: 'False to life and false to art' – a fitting introduction to the detective, American-born Astrogen Kerby, or Astro, who claims to be a palmist and crystal gazer. The clients whom he receives in his luxury flat and rescues from a number of dangerous and delicate situations are all of the utmost distinction.

Astrogen Kerby, alias Astro the clairvoyant, as an Indian Prince, with his mistress, Valeska Wynne, and a beautiful client, portrayed by George Brehm in 1912.

Nick Carter & Co.

Nick Carter first appeared in 'The New York Weekly' on 18 September 1886 in a story entitled *The Old Detective's Pupil*. The young man soon proved to be a gold mine, capable of filling a magazine of his own. The first writer to immortalize him in print was John Coryell, who was soon to be succeeded by Frederick van Renslaer Dey. Dey wrote more than a thousand Nick Carter stories and was very proud of his hero, who never smoked, drank, swore, or permitted a lie to pass his lips. 'I've never written a Nick Carter story I'd be ashamed to read to a Sunday School,' he once said.

In time Dey began to lose interest in his hero, and the stories were written by various freelance journalists at 50 to 100 dollars a time. Curiously enough, Carter made a come-back in 1964 in a novel entitled *Run Spy Run*, which was published anonymously. This involved bloodthirsty encounters with an agent of Communist China called Mr Judas, a gentleman with knives instead of fingers.

Nick Carter always had a false moustache in his pocket, and could transform himself with a turn of his jacket from a beggar to a prince.

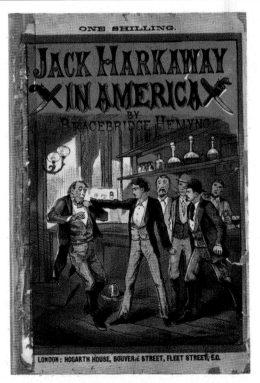

A generation ago Nick Carter was anathema to all pious critics of the entire genre; but though the moral tone of these shockers was considerably higher than their literary standard, they were, in fact, quite harmless.

...ARTER IN VARIOUS DISGUISES

Sexton Blake in mid-career, THE UNION JACK *(1915).*

England not only had, but still has, a detective capable of rivalling Nick Carter in popularity. Some years ago a schoolboy was asked in a radio quiz what famous detective lived in Baker Street. He replied without a moment's hesitation: 'Sexton Blake' – and he was right!

Sexton Blake holds the record for longevity. Since 1893 he has been in mortal danger at least once a week, but the experience has had no apparent effect on him, although he must be approaching eighty-five by now. Down the years hundreds of writers have written more than 200 million words on the exploits of this errand boy's Sherlock Holmes, and some of England's finest pens, it is rumoured, have contributed to his immortality. But no stylistic subtleties or ingenuities of plot confirm the rumour, and although a large printing is made of each number the publishers pay anything but princely fees.

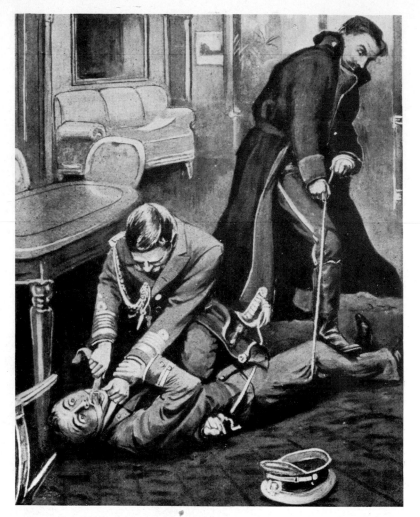

Illustration by Edward Read for Guy Boothby's A PRINCE OF SWINDLERS, *published a month or two before Grant Allen's* AN AFRICAN MILLIONAIRE *in 1897, and thus the first book to deal with a 'gentleman crook'.*

Above: the cover of E. Philips Oppenheim's book published in 1920 about the 'Diviner', Aaron Rodd, a typical scoundrel. Left: one of H. C. Greening's illustrations for JEFF PETERS AS A PERSONAL MAGNET, *one of the liveliest stories in O. Henry's classic,* THE GENTLE GRAFTER. *O. Henry, whose real name was William Sydney Porter, was born in North Carolina in 1862 and died in his 'Bagdad-on-the-Hudson', as he called New York. He had knocked about a lot, had spent three years in prison for embezzlement and in the last six years of his life he wrote a large number of incomparable stories about the people he had come to know on Broadway, in Harlem and on the East Side of the Hudson River – all of them the riff-raff and rejects of society.*

Confidence tricksters and charlatans

Crime literature deals with people ranging from murderers, blackmailers, kidnappers and violent robbers to petty thieves, confidence tricksters, unscrupulous financiers and venal detectives. E. W. Hornung's A. J. Raffles, who first appeared in 1899 in *The Amateur Cracksman*, is generally regarded as the first example in fiction of a gentleman crook. But the notion is wrong. Guy Boothby's Simon Carne made his début two years previously in *A Prince of Swindlers*, although how this interesting fact comes to be ignored by nearly everybody concerned with the history of the crime story is an unexplained mystery. For some years swindling was the popular game, and George Randolph Chester's four collections of short stories on the American 'business buccaneer', Get-Rich-Quick Wallingford (1908–13), and O. Henry's book, *The Gentle Grafter* (1908), were every bit as successful as the books of the twenties by William Le Queux, E. Phillips Oppenheim and Edgar Wallace with their gamblers, male and female, their bookmakers and their gentlemen crooks.

Here is a brief selection of typical stories dealing with the various categories of lesser criminals. CONFIDENCE TRICKSTERS: Christopher B. Booth's Amos Clackworthy in *Mr Clackworthy, Con Man* (New York, 1927); RASCALLY ATTORNEY: Melville Davisson Post's Randolph Mason (not to be confused with Perry M.!) in *The Strange Schemes of Randolph Mason* (New York, 1896); FORGER: R. Austin Freeman's Danby Croker in *The Exploits of Danby Croker* (London, 1916); SMUGGLER: William Hope Hodgson's *Captain Gault* (London, 1917); THIEF: Edgar Wallace's Anthony Smith in *The Mixer* (London, 1927); FEMALE THIEF: David Durham's (Roy Vickers') Fidelity Dove in *The Exploits of Fidelity Dove* (London, 1924); MARRIED COUPLE AS SWINDLERS: E. Phillips Oppenheim's Michael Sayers and his wife, Janet Soale, in *Michael's Evil Deeds* (London, 1924).

Above: 'Get-Rich-Quick Wallingford' in the congenial company of gamblers, as portrayed by F. R. Gruger. (From George Randolph Chester's YOUNG WALLINGFORD, *1910.)*

Bottom right: a trio of like-minded gentlemen. An illustration by H. C. Greening for O. Henry's memorable card-sharper story, INNOCENTS ON BROADWAY *(1908).*

Bottom left: Rasmus Christiansen's illustration for a story by the Danish writer, Johannes V. Jensen, written during his first visit the to US and published in 1906 in the Danish magazine 'Hjemmets Noveller' under the title HAN VAR FRA MISSOURI *(He Came from Missouri). Jensen also wrote a murder story,* FRU DOMINICK, *set on the steppes of Manchuria. Neither has been published in English.*

A modern Robin Hood

Leslie Charteris's Simon Templar, better known as 'The Saint', is generally regarded as the modern counterpart of the romantic, picaresque type of hero – always ready to go to the aid of women in distress and to deal with the villains baffling the police by methods that would certainly land him for years in jail if ever he were to be caught – which is of course unthinkable. Although Charteris made his début with *Enter the Saint* in 1928 at the age of twenty-one and is still writing as busily as ever, he is not quite as original as many people think. In essentials The Saint is a continuation of Sapper's (H. C. McNeile's) Bulldog Drummond, though the books also owe a lot to Dornford Yates and John Buchan. But Charteris is expert at giving a new twist to a theme, and the thrills in his latest books are set in all manner of countries. TV has done a lot to ensure the continued popularity of The Saint.

Sapper's Captain Hugh ('Bulldog') Drummond pictured at the height of his fame for 'The Strand Magazine'.

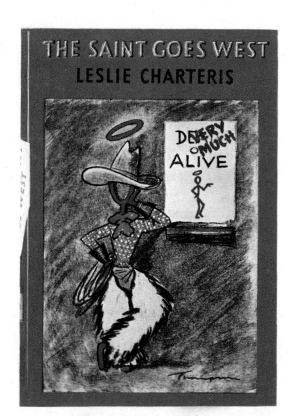

The sign of 'The Saint': a matchstick man crowned with a halo. His guises are endless: here he is seen as a wild-west cowboy.

One of the earliest 'noble robbers' in crime fiction was Constantine Dix, creation of the English writer, Barry Pain (1905).

Fantômas – the man with 100 faces – creation of the French writer, Allain Souvestre, is another noble-minded crook. A few years ago his adventures were filmed in colour and with considerable humour under the direction of André Hunebelle. Left: Rene Navarra as Fantômas in an early French version. Below: the journalist, Fandor (alias Fantômas), exchanging shots with Police Inspector Juve, who always manages to get the worst of it.

Jean Marais deals lovingly with Daniele Evenou in a film version of THE SAINT in a situation the author would never have put him in.

Bulldog Drummond has also been refilmed. In this version of DEADLIER THAN THE MALE Drummond is played by Richard Johnson, with Nigel Green as the villainous Carl Peterson, and Milton Reid as the muscular oriental bodyguard, Chang.

After Conan Doyle

*Arthur Morrison. A critic wrote of him:
Recommended when you are bored with
the family, worried over bills and sick
to death of problems.*

Following the success of Sherlock Holmes, England produced a long line of detectives.

Arthur Morrison (1863–1945) was one of the first with his private detective, Martin Hewitt. Hewitt had to be different from the bizarre Sherlock, of course, and Morrison achieved this by making him a very much more ordinary sort of person. Hewitt starts as a solicitor's clerk, a job which is instrumental in introducing him to his various experiences. This technique, which proved highly successful, goes back to Wilkie Collins, who first made a clerk into a detective in that splendid story, *A Plot in Private Life*. The Clerk, Mr Dark, a lively little man with an attractive double chin, searches the Scottish Highlands by horse and carriage for a missing bigamist. Like Hewitt, Dark is adept at making the most of his surroundings in order to get on a friendly footing with a stranger. His opening gambit is to praise the view of Edinburgh. Next he mentions whisky as the healthiest drink in the world. The third stage is to remember his beloved mother, not forgetting to add, now that he is in Scotland, that her maiden name was Macleod!

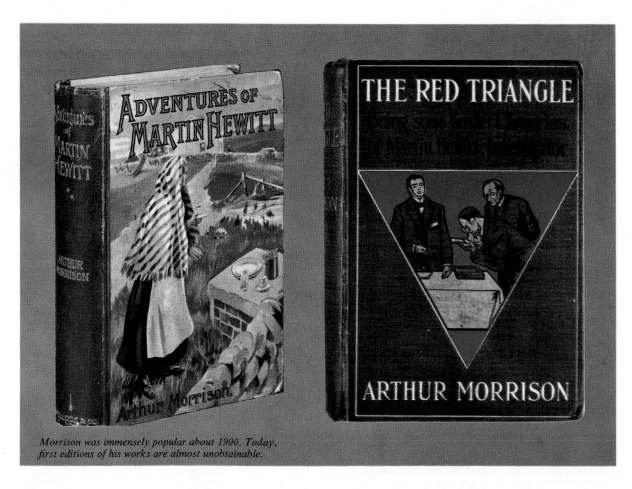

*Morrison was immensely popular about 1900. Today,
first editions of his works are almost unobtainable.*

A. E. W. Mason (1865–1948) does the precise opposite of Morrison. He out-Sherlocks Sherlock. His detective, a Frenchman, M. Hanaud, is even more arrogant than Holmes, and is accompanied at times by no less than two Watsons. He has a habit of breaking into sudden inconsequential laughter and, despite his corpulence, interrupts his investigations to do gymnastics with all the agility of an elephant. But despite the eccentricities of genius Hanaud is both shrewd and jovial, and all three of the Mason books in which he appears – *At the Villa Rose*, *The House of the Arrow* and *The Prisoner in the Opal* – can still be read with pleasure. The first, in particular, is a classic in structure. By page 15 of the book's 215 pages the murder has been committed; by page 135 Hanaud has cleared the murder up and the murder has been arrested. The rest of the book is devoted to explaining to the Dr Watsons and the reader that the girl was innocent, that the murderer changed the clues to point to an innocent person and that what really happened was . . . Hanaud, incidentally, is extremely gallant to the ladies – a virtue totally lacking in Holmes. The murder in *At the Villa Rose* occurs during a spiritualist seance – a feature that caused something of a stir at the time. Mason is one of the really enduring writers from the golden age of English detective story writing.

Above: Mason caricatured by Max Beerbohm. Right: Paget's illustration for Morrison's short story: THE QUINTON JEWEL AFFAIR.

The detective who got it wrong

E. C. Bentley (1875–1956) made his detective fall in love with the murdered man's widow and worked the romance into the complications of the plot.

This love interest was a novel feature at the time. Below: the widow, as portrayed in the first edition.

In 1913, at the dawn of England's golden age of detective writing, Edmund Clerihew Bentley published *Trent's Last Case*, a work which is reputed to have revolutionized the crime novel.

Like so many other writers in the genre, Bentley was a journalist and leader writer and in his lighter moments composed the four-line nonsense verses called clerihews after his second name. Bentley and Chesterton were close friends, though the story that Bentley wrote *Trent's Last Case* as the result of a bet between them is a myth.

In Chapter IX of his memoirs, *Those Days*, Bentley discusses *Trent's Last Case* and the thinking that lay behind it. But first he declares his attitude to Sherlock Holmes. There are two things about Holmes he does not much admire. One is the rich and complex character of the famous detective – in accordance with the Victorian fashion of creating 'rich characters' with eccentricities and peculiarities unlike any you meet in real life.

The other is the extreme seriousness of Holmes and his inability to take anything lightly. Bentley found this wearisome. It should be possible, he thought, to write a detective story in which the detective is recognizable as a human being and not so much the 'heavy' sleuth.

It was not until Bentley had gone a long way with his plot that the most pleasing notion of all came to him: that of making the hero's obviously correct solution of the mystery turn out to be completely wrong. Why not debunk the Sherlock Holmes myth of infallibility? Bentley decided to write an exposure of detective stories.

But 'the exposure' turned out to be a classic. It proved to be the starting signal for a whole host of realistic crime novels written in an attractively humorous style and with psychologically 'genuine' characterization.

The murdered man is a cold, neurotic American multi-millionaire named Sigsbee Manderson. 'It makes a good bill', says the Irish newspaper magnate of the placard announcing the death, as he sends one of his journalists, Trent, to cover the story, and it was Manderson's epitaph.

Five or six persons could have murdered him. After Trent has solved the mystery a further layer surrounding it proves him wrong, and then – a final and unrivalled shock effect – yet another layer proves that wrong too.

Trent is not alone on the job. There is also Mr Murch of Scotland Yard. 'He was as good as he was large, and he was large even by police standards,' says Bentley, with his customary lightness of touch.

Bentley followed up his first story of Trent's last case with two more Trent books. Unlike other critics, we consider them also to be excellent, even if they do break no fresh ground.

Bentley's novel as a film: Michael Wilding (right) as Trent, Margaret Lockwood as the widow – Orson Welles, incidentally, was the tycoon, her husband – and Miles Malleson (left) as the murderer. (Directed by Herbert Wilcox.)

A galaxy of detectives portrayed by the Danish cartoonist, Storm-P.; but Trent, unfortunately, is not among them.

Monsieur Arsène Lupin

Arsène Lupin, the gentleman crook, was well endowed with graces by his creator; chief among them was his Gallic sense of humour. Left: Lupin, as Leo Fontain, the artist, imagined him in LES TROIS CRIMES D'ARSÈNE LUPIN *(1910). Below: for once Lupin has landed in jail, but of course he soon escapes.*

man *Cambrioleur* (1907) that we first hear of this extraordinary character, Lupin. The passage runs: 'What is he like? How shall I put it? I've seen Arsène Lupin perhaps twenty times, and each time he's been different. Only his eyes, his figure, and his bearing have been the same. "I scarcely know who I am myself," he once said. "Sometimes I don't recognize the person I see before me in the mirror. But why should I always be the same? If I were, I could no longer move about as freely as I like. My actions tell all that needs to be told about me. I don't need the appearance of any set personality. So much the better if no-one can take me by the scruff of the neck and say: this is Arsène Lupin."'

Boothby's Simon Carne and Allen's Colonel Clay, 'the African millionaire', have already been mentioned as the first gentlemen crooks in fiction. While they are both now forgotten, E. W. Hornung's cricketing hero, Raffles, and Maurice Leblanc's Arsène Lupin still attract readers.

At the turn of the century there was a considerable difference in British and French moral attitudes. If a man in an English crime novel had a mistress, the reader could count on his being one of the villains. A man similarly placed in a corresponding French book, however, would most probably be found in the opposite camp. If British sympathies were to be roused in favour of a rascal he had at least to be a sportsman and, if necessary, ready to lay down his life for his country. It is in *Arsène Lupin, Gentle-*

Maurice Leblanc (1864–1941) was a journalist, and in 1906 was commissioned to write a crime story for 'Je Sais Tout'. This led to the creation of Arsène Lupin, whose fame depends in part on his several encounters with Sherlock Holmes, whom the author took the precaution of calling 'Herlock Sholmes'. In a long career ending only in the thirties, Lupin was the brain behind a long series of robberies which had the police completely baffled.

In the collection of short stories, LES HUIT COUPS DE L'HORLOGE *(1922), Leblanc made his gentleman crook play the role of detective under the name of Prince Serge Renine. This illustration showing him at work is by G. W. Gage for the American edition.*

G. K. Chesterton once toyed with the idea of Gaston Leroux's being a *nom de plume* for Maurice Leblanc. 'There would', he said, 'be something very symmetrical in the inversion by which the red gentleman always writes about a detective, and the white gentleman always writes about a criminal.

'But I have no serious reason to suppose the red and white combination to be anything but a coincidence; and the tales are of two rather different types. Those of Gaston the Red are more strictly of the type of the mystery story, in the sense of resolving a single and central mystery. Those of Maurice the White are more properly adventure stories, in the sense of resolving a rapid succession of immediate difficulties. This is inherent in the position of the hero; the detective is always outside the event, while the criminal is inside the event.

'Some would express it by saying that the policeman is always outside the house when the burglar is inside the house.'

That definition is one most readers would probably accept, and, coming at a moment when we are considering the different forms the popular crime novel can take, is well-timed.

Arsène Lupin at the age of twenty in
LA DUCHESSE DE CAGLIOSTRO.
He has yet to become a
'gentleman' but nonetheless looks
astonishingly like a youthful
Maurice Chevalier.

Mr A. J. Raffles

The gentleman crook,
A. J. Raffles, in action under the eye of
his 'Watson', Bunny Manders.
Illustration by
Cyrus Cuneo, 1905.

While the Sherlock Holmes stories were at the height of their success, Conan Doyle's brother-in-law, E. W. Hornung, agreed to write a series of detective stories seen from the other side of the fence. These described the exploits of a gentleman crook, A. J. Raffles, whose biographer, Bunny Manders, is constantly warning him of the dangers and trying, in vain, to make him return to the security of a respectable mode of existence. Like his French colleague, Arsène Lupin, Raffles does an occasional spell as a detective. But he does not make a very convincing one; crime seems to be very much more in his line.

In a collection of short stories, *The Amateur Cracksman* (1899), Raffles is presented as a famous cricketer of good family and, apparently, of some means. But his means derive from the daring robberies he indulges in each time his funds are getting low. There are, of course, limits to how far an author can go in describing the career of a romantic adventurer like Raffles without losing the sympathy of his readers, and the career of Raffles was comparatively short. The first volume had no more than two sequels: *Raffles* (1901) and *A Thief in the Night* (1905), the latter ending with the heroic death of Raffles in the Boer War.

Hornung also wrote a single detective novel: *The Crime Doctor* (1914).

Rome, 1905: E. W. Hornung (1866–1921), left, photographed with his brother-in-law, Arthur Conan Doyle, and H. G. Wells.

A detective with his own laboratory

In 1907 a notable advance was made in the detective novel with the invention by an English writer, R. Austin Freeman (1862–1943), of the 'scientific' detective in the person of Dr John Thorndyke, an expert in forensic medicine in some kind of semi-official position. Freeman was himself interested in science, and used to try out his plots in his own laboratory, so much so that the police themselves adopted some of his methods. In the first Dr Thorndyke book, *The Red Thumb Mark*, a red thumb print is discovered in the box from which some diamonds have disappeared. It belongs to the nephew of the owner of the diamonds, so it is taken for granted that he must be guilty of stealing them. But the detective can prove otherwise. Dr Thorndyke subsequently appeared in a long list of novels (the best, in our opinion, being *Mr Pottermack's Oversight* (1930)), and in short stories. They all remain excellent reading.

Left: illustration by H. M. Brock for the short story, THE BLUE SEQUIN *(1909). A young actress is found murdered in a first-class compartment. Dr Thorndyke is summoned by wire.*

The detective and his assistant give Professor Poppelbaum a lesson in Thorndyke's residence, 5A King's Bench Walk, an address which became almost as famous as 221B Baker Street.

Above: typical illustration from a Thorndyke story: a photomicrograph of sand taken from the pillow of a murdered woman.

Below: unknown artist's impression of Dr Thorndyke, who not only prophesied the scientific method but also strongly criticized the attitude of the police to suspects and their treatment of them on remand.

The 'inverted' story

The detective surprised in his laboratory. One of Freeman's many collections of cases featuring Dr Thorndyke.

Left: before Freeman became famous in 1907, he and another writer collaborated under the pseudonym of Clifford Ashdown in writing a not particularly successful collection of stories entitled THE ADVENTURES OF ROMNEY PRINGLE *(1902). The detective genre has some of the world's keenest book collectors, but so far they have been able to find only six copies of the book.*

Freeman gave a new twist to the genre. He introduced the 'inverted' story. This starts by describing the crime, next gives the solution of the mystery, and only then moves on to the work of detection. The advantages of this break in one of the taboos of the genre were obvious. In the first place the reader could study the culprit and consider his mentality and motives for committing the crime. After that he could devote his whole attention to the sleuth. Freeman's first experiment with this promising innovation was *The Singing Bone* (1912). But the writer who exploited it most successfully was Anthony Berkeley Cox. As 'Anthony Berkeley' he wrote several witty detective novels, the best known being *The Poisoned Chocolates Case* (1929) and *Trial and Error* (1937), both extremely readable. Under the pseudonym of Francis Iles he produced the outstanding work in the 'inverted story' genre: *Before the Fact* (1932). In this the name of the murderer is revealed in the second sentence! The rest of the book tells how the murder is planned – with the victim's knowledge!

Others who use the device effectively are Richard Hull and, in particular, Roy Vickers.

Two more scientific detectives:

Above: T. S. Stribling's Paggioli, in
CLUES OF THE CARRIBEES *(1929). Paggioli
is a psychologist.*

*The genre has many of the breed – from
psychoanalysts to psychiatrists.*

*The mental processes of murderers are
gradually becoming more and more complex. Frank Heller gave his Freudian
psychologist the revealing name of Dr
Zimmertür.*

*Right: an American classic. Craig Ken-
nedy, professor of chemistry, covers the
villain with his revolver in* THE TERROR IN
THE AIR. *The three men accompanying him
are members of Pinkerton's famous staff.
The man in the background is the chroni
cler, journalist Walter Jameson.*

*Reeves was at one time as popular as
Doyle, but the dust of history has now
settled on him. Illustration: Will Foster.*

The wisdom of Father Brown

Father Brown in his innocence is so ordinary – which is what is so out-of-the-ordinary about him. It is as if Gilbert Keith Chesterton wanted to prove that a detective does not need to have an aquiline profile and a pipe, or a monocle and deerstalker hat, in order to be a character. Father Brown's mild, effacing manner, reflected in his chubby face, are such pronounced characteristics that no reader can fail to register the appearance of his hero.

If one regards the detective story purely as escapist literature – as indeed one should – one might expect the ethics of Father Brown and the propagandist tendencies of Chesterton to be a serious handicap. The fact that they are not is because Chesterton is the greatest paradox-monger and one of the most important writers ever to write a detective story. Chesterton was also the first critic of consequence brave enough to defend the genre publicly. He did so in 1901 – before he had written a detective story himself – in an essay entitled *A Defence of Detective Stories*. Since then he has defended and delineated the charm of detective literature so often that there is a Chesterton reply to any question on the subject an enquiring interviewer might think up.

Father Brown is the type of detective the critics label 'intuitive', meaning that he obtains his results by an immediate appreciation of the totality and context of a case, and not by logical thinking. Howard Haycraft goes so far as to describe the *metaphysical* detective story as Chesterton's most important contribution to the genre. But the fact that the kind of apparently supernatural conundrums that confront us in e.g. *The Hammer of God* and *The Invisible Man* can be solved and be shown to be purely natural ones, indicates that there is nothing metaphysical about them. (In this connection interested readers are referred to Algernon Blackwood's *John Silence* and William Hope Hodgson's *Carnacki, the Ghost-Finder*.) We cannot recall any instance of Chesterton, even at his most paradoxical, ever failing to keep his feet on the ground. Spirituality is kept for the concluding moral.

Two photographs from Chesterton's AUTOBIOGRAPHY *(1936), showing him aged fifteen or sixteen, and as the world-famous writer.*

The first collection of Father Brown stories, THE INNOCENCE OF FATHER BROWN, *was published in 1911 with illustrations by Sidney Seymour Lucas. The next volume,* THE WISDOM OF FATHER BROWN *(1914) contained this coloured frontispiece, showing the priest in the witness box from the story* THE MAN IN THE PASSAGE.

Chesterton was often caricatured – and liked it, even when it was as unkind as this representation of 'the paradox-monger'.

Monsignor Ronald Knox, himself no mean detective writer, says in his introduction to The World's Classics edition of *Father Brown* that Chesterton wanted to create a detective as unlike Lord Peter Wimsey as possible. If this was so then there was indeed something metaphysical about Chesterton, for the first Father Brown stories were published in 'The Saturday Evening Post' some ten years before Dorothy L. Sayers had even thought of bringing Lord Peter into the world. Anyone reading Chesterton's essays on crime literature will also realize that he had no desire for his detective to detract from any of the great detectives already existing, all of whom he could appreciate better than most. Chesterton was simply incapable of creating a figure like anyone else – not even like John O'Connor, the original model for Father Brown, of whom Chesterton says: 'I permitted myself the grave liberty of taking my friend and knocking him about; beating his hat and umbrella shapeless, untidying his clothes, punching his intelligent countenance into a condition of pudding-faced fatuity...'

G. K. Chesterton's other detectives and Father Brown in films

Father Brown observing, as Sidney Seymour Lucas depicted him in THE SINS OF PRINCE SARADINE *from* THE INNOCENCE OF FATHER BROWN *(1911). That ever popular theme, the duel, plays an important role and Flambeau, the master thief, is presented in a favourable light.*

Heinz Rühmann, the German actor, was one of the screen's most faithful representations of Father Brown. Here he is seen in DAS SCHWARZE SCHAFF *(The Black Cupboard).*

Between 1911 and 1935 G.K.Chesterton wrote five collections of Father Brown stories, but never put him in a novel. Those short stories, however, were not his sole contribution to crime literature. There was an earlier collection in 1905, *The Club of Queer Trades*, in which Chesterton himself played a kind of Watson role to a former judge, Basil Grant. Chesterton also illustrated the book with thirty-two amusing drawings.

This was followed in 1908 by *The Man Who Was Thursday*, a work which with a little goodwill could also be classed as a crime novel, although in reality it is a philosophical farce in which the members of a secret anarchist society prove to belong to the secret police.

Other detectives were Gabriel Gase in *The Poet and the Lunatics* (1929) and Horne Fisher in *The Man Who Knew Too Much* (1933).

Four Faultless Felons appeared in 1930; finally there is the somewhat dry and paradoxical figure of Mr Pond, a detective bearing no more than a slight resemblance to his author (and Father Brown), in *The Paradoxes of Mr Pond*, which was published in 1937, the year after Chesterton's death.

Probably both Chesterton and Brown took a far more compassionate view of Flambeau, the master-

criminal, than the representatives of the official police did. Human nature and ethical problems were what interested Chesterton, and it is a pity he never wrote a crime play. His powers as a dramatist were amply demonstrated in 1911 in his splendid comedy, *Magic*.

Chesterton himself drew the illustrations for THE CLUB OF QUEER TRADES *(1905). A dramatic scene from the book.*

Crime fiction and real life crime

Real life crimes have of course been a frequent source of inspiration to crime writers. Poe, for example, based *The Murders in the Rue Morgue* and *The Mystery of Marie Rogêt* on incidents from real life, and Ellery Queen set Sherlock Holmes the mystery of Jack the Ripper to solve. In an appendix to the anthology *Murder Plain and Fanciful* James Sandoe gives 207 similar examples prior to 1948. Since then there have been as many more, so we can hardly give more than a brief selection here. Marie Belloc Lowndes was the first to put Jack the Ripper into a novel, and *The Lodger* (1913) is still regarded as one of the best thrillers ever written. Thomas Burke also used the Ripper in his famous short story, *The Hands of Mr Ottermole* (1931), while Robert Bloch, in *Yours Truly, Jack the Ripper* (1945), tried to present a really original solution to the problem. Then the Lizzie Borden case is one of the most interesting and mysterious in US legal history. In 1892, despite overwhelming proof, this young woman was acquitted of having axed her parents to death. As early as 1895 Mary E. Wilkins used the theme in *The Long Arm*, and ten years later Lily Dougall did the same in *The Summit House Mystery*. But these stories are far less interesting than the psychological studies of Lizzie by Marie Belloc in *Lizzie Borden, a Study in Conjecture* (1930) and Edward Hale Bierstadt in *Satan was a Man* (1935). Lizzie Borden's fate has often been dramatized. The first time was in 1933. Then there was a radio play based on the case which was broadcast by the BBC on 16 July 1945. The author, Donald Henderson, kept strictly to the facts – unlike Lilian de la Torre in her thriller, *Goodbye, Miss Lizzie Borden* (1948), although she managed to be more exciting

The fate of Eugene Aram, who was hanged in 1777 for a murder committed fifteen years previously, has inspired several writers. Thomas Hood's book, THE DREAM OF EUGENE ARAM, THE MURDERER *(1831), was based on his life, and Bulwer-Lytton wrote a tear-jerker novel about him.*

Mrs Belloc Lowndes, author of THE LODGER. *The book was filmed in 1926 by Alfred Hitchcock with Ivor Novello as the mysterious lodger suspected of being Jack the Ripper*

When Mary
Nicholls, Jack
the Ripper's
third victim, was
murdered, the
newspapers
published 'authentic
pictures' from the
scene of the crime.

Constance Kent, the accused in the famous 'Road Case', appears –
so far as the facts of the case go – in both Wilkie Collins's THE
MOONSTONE (1868), and, under the name of Valentine North, in
Mary Hayley Bell's play, ANGEL. In this play, which was first
presented in Liverpool on 12 May 1947, the author departed from
fact only in the introduction of a love interest.

Lizzie Borden, photographed shortly before her parents were
murdered in their home at Fall River. A contemporary verse
reported cynically:

Lizzie Borden took an axe
And gave her mother forty whacks
And when she saw what she had done
She gave her father forty-one.

Real life crime in modern crime writing

The picture above shows Laird Cregar in *The Lodger*, the Twentieth Century Fox film of Mrs Belloc Lowndes's novel (1944). For good reasons this could only give a fictional solution to the Jack the Ripper mystery, and until recent years crime writers were chary of using real crimes without shrouding them in a more or less impenetrable smoke screen. One or two exceptions that come to mind are Miriam Allen de Ford's *Homecoming* (1935), based on the lynching of J. M. Holmes and Thomas Thurmond in November 1933 for the murder of Brooke Hart in San José, California, and Theodore Dreiser's *An American Tragedy* (1926).

This classic example reproduced parts of the trial of Chester Gillette for the murder of Grace Brown at Big Moose Lake, Airondacks in 1906, word for word. Gillette is the Clyde Griffiths of the novel. Aldous Huxley's famous short story, *The Gioconda Smile*, from the collection entitled *Mortal Coils* (1922), contained important features of the Greenwood poison case, as the author admitted, while Upton Sinclair's *Boston* (1928), is based on the Sacco-Vanzetti case of 1920. The two men were condemned on inadequate evidence, although according to latest research that is not to say that they were innocent of the double murder with which they were charged.

Apart from Truman Capote's masterpiece, *In Cold Blood*, Meyer Levin's *Compulsion* (1957) is one of the most recent examples of the perfect 'crime fact' novel. According to the foreword the book is based on the Leopold and Loeb case of May, 1924, in which two teenagers, the sons of wealthy fathers, murdered fourteen-year-old Bobby Franks out of pure sadism and to show that they could commit 'the perfect crime'. They were condemned to life imprisonment. Loeb was stabbed during homosexual prison riots in 1936. Leopold was pardoned in 1958 and now lives in Puerto Rico.

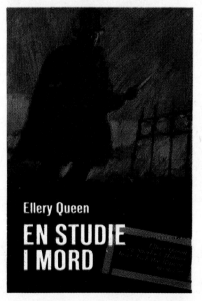

Meyer Levin's COMPULSION
*was filmed with Dean Stockwell,
Bradford Dillman and Orson Welles
in the main roles.*

*Two modern illustrators
have much the same conception of Jack the
Ripper. Left: the cover of the Danish
version of Ellery Queen's* A STUDY IN
TERROR, *and an English paperback of*
THE LODGER *by Marie Belloc Lowndes.*

Tom Sawyer and other boy detectives

With young people so enthusiastic about crime literature it is surprising there have not been more boy detectives in crime fiction. It might, of course, be objected that few children clear up crimes in real life, but haven't we all pretended to be Sherlock Holmes or Nick Carter at some time in our lives?

Mark Twain's *Tom Sawyer, Detective* (1896) was the first book in the genre and remains the best. Tom and his friend, Huck Finn, get to the bottom of a murder and receive 2,000 dollars in reward. Tom, incidentally, is so precocious that he uses fingerprints, while Mark Twain appears to have lifted the 'murder' together with one or two minor details from a short story, *The Vicar of Vejlbye* (Præsten i Vejlbye) by the Danish writer, Steen Steensen Blicher. The story was pub-

Bottom left: Tom Sawyer, proud detective, as depicted by A. B. Frost for the first edition. Above: a dramatic scene as Roy Fuller's Frederick Trench is chased by a dragon in female form. Drawing by Roger Payne for WITH MY LITTLE EYE *(1948).*

lished in 1826 and immediately translated into German.

In 1915 an English and an American boy both started careers as detectives. The English boy, Lord Frederic Hamilton's J. P. Davenant, was a typical upper-class teenager and appeared in four collections of short stories published during the First World War, so naturally he became a secret agent. Hervey J. O'Higgins's Barney Cook, whose exploits are described in *The Adventures of Detective Barney*, is treated more humorously, although his adventures and discoveries are worthy of a fully fledged detective. In the forties Ellery Queen let his amateur detective's young servant, Djuna, take over seven of his cases.

Right: the boy detective, J. P. Davenant, in an 'authentic' photograph. Below: a strip cartoon by John T. McCutcheon with a boy detective as the super-hero in a delightful collection of parodies, BANG! BANG! *(1928), by George Ade.*

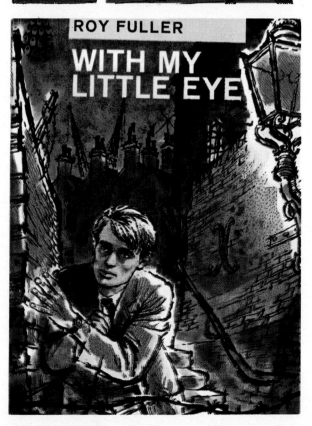

Roger Payne's cover for a paperback edition of WITH MY LITTLE EYE, *by the English writer, Roy Fuller.*

Robert Arthur's series about three boy detectives, Bob Andrews, Pete Crenshaw and Jupiter Jones, has been a big success. The involvement of Alfred Hitchcock has no doubt helped.

Above: Watson and Holmes in a train. Illustration by Sidney Paget. Below: a scene from the classic, IN THE FOG, by Richard Harding Davis.

Homage to a railway engineer

'There's a train from Paddington at 11.15.' And Dr Watson in his bowler and Sherlock Holmes in his deerstalker are off to solve another mystery. Trains are as popular in the detective genre as the hansom cab. Even Gaboriau's detectives go by train. Bram Stoker in his thriller, *Dracula*, was probably the first to introduce that romantic centre piece of so many mysteries, the Balkan Express, into his plot. But these two pages are chiefly meant as a tribute to Freeman Wills Crofts (1879–1957), who was a trained railway engineer. With timetables and maps beside him he constructed novels so ingeniously that the person with the most cast-iron alibi often turned out to be the one who was guilty.

Crofts (left) became an author by chance. He wrote his first book, THE CASK, *in 1919 while convalescing, and only realized later that he had potentialities as a writer outside the sickroom.* THE CASK *was a big success and is still extremely readable to this day.*

Crofts' detectives have always been police inspectors from Scotland Yard, working at times with their colleagues in the Paris Sûreté. One of his favourite tricks is to let the amateurs flounder about in the first half of the book. Then the professionals enter the scene and bring science to bear on the problem. There is an example of this in that excellent book, *The Pit Prop Syndicate*, with its painstaking Inspector Willis of the C.I.D., and there is another in *The Cheyne Mystery*, Crofts' best book, in which his most famous detective, Inspector French, unravels the tangled threads of the affair. French is diligence and thoroughness personified and, despite his deliberate tempo, is fascinating to follow.

It has been suggested that French was the model for Simenon's Maigret. Like Maigret he has a loyal wife at home who is ready to listen to him and share his silences. Unlike Maigret, though, he has no inner life.

The great charm of Crofts lies in his *construction*.

Francis Iles's 'inverted' crime story, BEFORE THE FACT, *filmed by Hitchcock with Cary Grant and Joan Fontaine.*

One of the world's most popular writers

Agatha Christie was born in Torquay in 1890. Her father, Frederick Alvah Miller, was an American. Agatha was still a child when he died, so she was brought up by her broad-minded mother, who with their neighbour, Eden Phillpotts, the writer, encouraged her to write at an early age. In 1914, soon after the outbreak of war, Agatha Mary Clarissa Miller married a young flying officer, Archibald Christie, later Colonel Christie, C.M.G., D.S.O. When he was ordered to France his wife immediately joined the Red Cross, where she was put in charge of the hospital poison cupboard. Its thrilling contents fascinated her to such a degree that she began to study toxicology in the library and soon knew all that there was worth knowing about dosages and the effect of poisons. 'Give me a decent bottle of poison', she remarked one day, 'and I'll construct the perfect crime.' At the end of the war she planned a detective novel.

'I had read many good detective stories,' she says, 'and I'd found them an excellent way of forgetting your troubles.' She discussed the project with her sister, who said she couldn't imagine a *good* detective story where it was impossible to know at once who had committed the crime. 'I said I thought I could write one, and thus spurred I wrote *The Mysterious Affair at Styles*.'

Hercule Poirot as depicted by W. Smithson Broadhead for 'The Weekly Sketch', which published the first Poirot stories in the twenties. The series appeared in book form in 1924 as POIROT INVESTIGATES. *Poirot, who has retired from a high position in the Belgian police, has moved with war refugees to England and, after meeting his 'Watson', Captain Arthur Hastings, sets up as a private detective in London.*

Mrs Christie often accompanies her husband to archaeological excavations. This picture by Professor Jørgen Læssøe was taken at Nimrud, Iraq.

Bottom: Hercule Poirot on the cover of a modern paperback. He has appeared in one film only, THE ALPHABET MURDERS, *based on the novel,* THE A.B.C. MURDERS. *Tony Randall played the detective, and is seen here in a somewhat ludicrous position.*

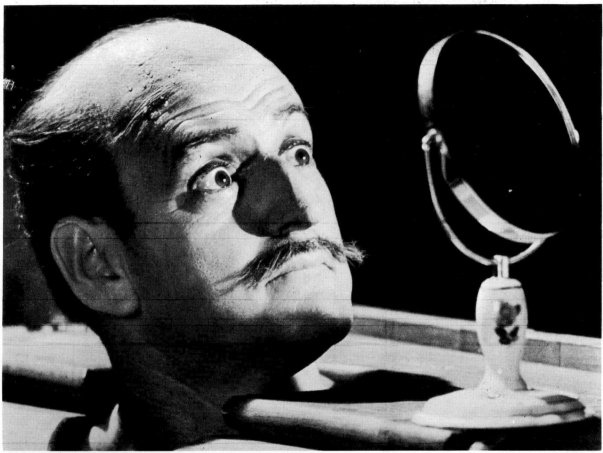

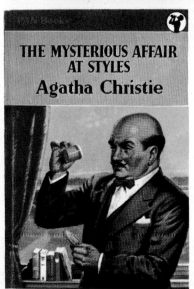

THE MYSTERIOUS AFFAIR AT STYLES
Agatha Christie

The first Poirot novel did not find an immediate publisher. Six times the manuscript was returned with the usual: 'We have read your book with interest but regret . . .'. It was only after peace had been signed and Mrs Christie's only daughter had been born that, on the initiative of John Lane, the work appeared in print. He chose to publish it in New York, and it achieved a modest success – enough, though, to encourage the author to persevere, and, fortunately for Mr Lane, she had bound herself to let him have her next four books on terms particularly advantageous – to him. But it was six years before a best-seller came her way with *The Murder of Roger Ackroyd* – a *tour de force* which provoked a violent discussion, with members of the old school crying 'Cheat', and other readers and critics rallying to the author's side, declaring it was up to the reader to suspect *everybody*.

Production then got really going, with two new books a year. Today Agatha Christie is one of the world's most popular writers, with no less than fifty-eight crime novels and nineteen collections of short stories to her credit. And she marked her eightieth birthday by producing her eightieth book.

Miss Marple and Monsieur Poirot

Agatha Christie gradually began to tire of Poirot and now prefers her other detective, Miss Jane Marple, the lovable spinster from the idyllic village of St Mary Mead. Miss Marple was first presented as a slight figure in fichu and lace, but nowadays she is identified by a much larger public with the bulkier, energetic figure of Margaret Rutherford, who has played her in four successful films. In *Murder at the Gallop*, the film based on the book, *After the Funeral*, Miss Marple stepped right into the shoes of Hercule Poirot.

The Danish graphic artist, Lars Bo, drew this charming silhouette of Poirot in 1954.

If in Shaftesbury Avenue one day you were to meet a slight, elderly gentleman, rather overdressed by English standards, with an egg-shaped head and a face embellished with an enormous waxed moustache, you would no doubt instantly recognize him as M. Hercule Poirot – only to realize immediately afterwards that the figure who is almost as familiar to you as Sherlock Holmes only exists in the imagination of a fiendishly gifted woman writer. And yet the encounter could have occurred. Agatha Christie herself relates how once when lunching at the Savoy Hotel she saw him sitting at the table beside hers: a small man with the same pomaded moustache, egg-shaped head and, apparently, the same well-developed little grey cells. The likeness was so striking that Mrs Christie could not help exclaiming: 'Why, it *is* him!' And when she remarked on it to the head-waiter she found that he had noticed the likeness too, and could tell her that the elegant gentleman was in fact a Belgian residing in London.

Referring to Miss Marple, Mrs Christie says that she has something in common with her own grandmother – also a pink and white old lady – who, despite her sheltered Victorian existence, always had a very clear idea of the depths of human wickedness.

Dorothy L. Sayers and the aristocratic detective

Peter Wimsey, Dorothy L. Sayers' detective, is a complete contrast to the dandified, meticulous Poirot, who certainly does not include modesty among his virtues. Nor does Lord Peter, for that matter, though in his case it is because he never thinks about it, any more than he wonders whether people notice his clothes, which are of course from the best tailor in Saville Row and so have built-in distinction. His entry in 'Who's Who' runs: WIMSEY, Peter Death Bredon (Lord), D.S.O., born 1890; second *s.* of Mortimer Gerald Bredon Wimsey, 15th Duke of Denver, and Honoria Lucasta, *d.* of Francis Delagardi of Bellingham Manor, Bucks. *Educ.* Eton College and Balliol College, Oxford. Served War of 1914–18 (Major, Rifle Brigade). *Publications*: 'Notes for Collectors of Incunabula', 'The Murderer's Compendium', etc. *Recreations*: Criminology, books, music, cricket. *Clubs*: Marlborough, Egoists'. *Address*: 110A Piccadilly, W. 1.; Bredon Hall, Duke's Denver, Norfolk. *Arms*: Sable, three mice rampant argent; helmet: cat crouchant in natural colours; motto: As my wimsey takes me.

The short stories of Dorothy L. Sayers are to be found in three books: LORD PETER VIEWS THE BODY *(1928),* HANGMAN'S HOLIDAY *(1933), and* IN THE TEETH OF THE EVIDENCE *(1933). These collections contain eighteen Wimsey stories, twelve stories featuring the wine agent and amateur detective, Montagu Egg, and twelve mystery stories. Two Peter Wimsey stories appear in anthologies only: the chess mystery,* STRIDING FOLLY, *and the adventure of* THE HAUNTED POLICEMAN, *in which Lord Peter on the very night that his wife gives birth to a healthy baby boy, gets involved in a most unusual mystery.*

A typical illustration from 'Pearson's Magazine' of Lord Peter and his nephew in THE DRAGON'S HEAD.

Dorothy Leigh Sayers (1893–1957) was the daughter of a clergyman in an attractive part of East Anglia, a district which forms the background to *The Nine Tailors* (1934), one of the most original detective novels ever written. She read the history of literature at Somerville College, Oxford, and with her M.A. in 1915 was one of the first women to gain a degree at that university. After some years with an advertising agency in London she was sufficiently independent financially to maintain herself as a writer. These brief biographical details serve to indicate where Dorothy Sayers got the inspiration for *Gaudy Night* (1935) and *Murder Must Advertise* (1933). Her writing gradually changed from pure detective writing with a good murder as the central feature to interest in the activities of Lord Peter and the almost divinely unattainable Harriet Vane. Dorothy Sayers also wrote various essays on crime fiction, e.g. a painstaking historical introduction to the anthology, *Great Stories of Mystery, Detection and Imagination*, more than a million copies of which have been printed since it first appeared in 1928, and five dissertations on Sherlock Holmes, which were printed in different periodicals and are now available in her *Unpopular Opinions* (1946).

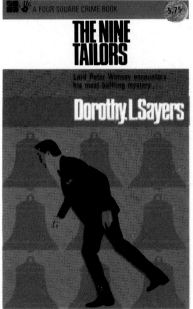

The dust-jackets to the first editions of Dorothy L. Sayers scarcely merit reproduction. We prefer the covers of the paperback editions of her two most famous stories: MURDER MUST ADVERTISE *and* THE NINE TAILORS, *both of which are read as enthusiastically today as nearly a generation ago, despite the contempt felt by fans of the hard-boiled school for the snobbish genre she represented.*

113

Edgar Wallace (1875–1932) was born in Greenwich, the illegitimate son of an actress, who placed him out with a fishporter's wife in Billingsgate, where he grew up with her ten children. 'Dick Freeman', as he was known then, was a lively lad, sold newspapers, worked for a bookprinter, as a ship's boy and an errand boy, thus gaining an intimate knowledge of London. Leaving school at twelve he went on educating himself, joined the army and spent seven years in South Africa. There he wrote poems, became a correspondent for Reuters, and, on returning to England, joined the 'Daily Mail'. Soon, however, he was sued for libel and dismissed. He was always a gambler and always in debt, and was desperate when he wrote his first thriller, *The Four Just Men*. This became a best-seller, and when in 1911 he began the series *Sanders of the River* his fame was secure. His output became prolific. In 1928 every fourth novel sold in England was his. In the course of twenty-seven years he published some 150 novels, though that is not to say that he wrote merely in order to live as a *grand seigneur*. His knowledge of the underworld of London and its slang was profound and is admirably described in his many admittedly melodramatic novels featuring rascally financiers, innocent girls, Chinese villains, gentleman thieves, racing sharks and master criminals.

Vignette advertising a modern Edgar Wallace film.

A single company, Rialto/Constantin, has made more than twenty Wallace films in recent years. All have been successful. Below: Stewart Granger as Police Inspector Cooper Smith in THE TRYGON FACTOR.

Above: the most famous of all photographs of Edgar Wallace, taken at the height of his fame. Below: the first edition of Wallace's best collection of detective stories, THE MIND OF MR J. G. REEDER *(1926).*

When Wallace died he left debts of over £200,000, but within a few years his estate was showing a profit.

The most famous of his books was *The Crimson Circle* (1922); only a few of them are detective stories proper. The best are those about the 'silent detective', Oliver Rater, known as the Orator, from Scotland Yard, and the embarrassed, taciturn Mr J. Reeder, very polite and correct in his speech, with old-fashioned mutton-chop whiskers, a cravat, a habit of pushing his spectacles up on his forehead when he reads, and an umbrella which remains resolutely unopened whatever the weather. Human passions do not affect him. As he remarks to a romantic police constable: 'Love is a very great experience – I've just read about it.'

115

Why murder
is the popular crime

Above: drawing by Frederic Dorr Steele for Davis's IN THE FOG.
Below: scene from an E. Phillips Oppenheim story.

Most crime novels are concerned with murder and the hunt for the murderer. This is the theme of the next four pages.

Why is murder so popular as a crime? There are many theories. Dorothy L. Sayers, for example, writes: 'Death in particular seems to provide the minds of the Anglo-Saxon race with a greater fund of innocent amusement than any other single subject . . . Let the murder turn out to be no murder, but a mere accident or suicide, and letters pour in from indignant readers. . . . The tale must be about dead bodies or very wicked people, preferably both, before the Tired Business Man can feel really happy and at peace with the world.'

Dorothy Sayers loved to provoke people. Still, suppose you were to examine your own attitude – where would you stand? Make a list of your ten favourite novels and then see how many of them contain a murder. About ninety per cent with a murder appears to be about normal. 'The tale must be about dead bodies – before people can be at peace!'

'At this instant I flung open one of the shutters, and simultaneously I heard a cry of horror from my clerk.' Illustration from about 1875 in one of Allan Pinkerton's many books on dramatic and deadly crimes. Pinkerton launched them as true stories based on reports from Pinkerton's National Detective Bureau. Note the blood on the carpet.

The man with the gun is not the murderer but Philip Marlowe, the detective. The scene is from Raymond Chandler's first novel, THE BIG SLEEP. The film-script writers included William Faulkner, the director was Howard Hawks, while the part of the impudent, hard-boiled Marlowe was played with superb irony by Humphrey Bogart.

117

The victim, the flight and the hunt

Two novels immediately spring to mind under this heading as being particularly worth recommending.

One is *Roparen*, the most important work of a Swedish writer, Stieg Trenter. In this book not only is the murderer different from the person we thought, but so is the victim too!

Though women frequently figure as the victims or villains in crime stories, the more rewarding role of detective is usually reserved to men. But in Trenter's book a girl is both victim and villain: a chameleon whose colour changes as the novel progresses.

It is all done with a masterly hand. Trenter's book would merit a place in the most select international company.

The other book we would mention in this connection is Geoffrey Household's *Rogue Male*.

This has something of the pursuit element so characteristic of the special agent novel about it. But there are differences. The main character starts by being the pursuer. His hobby is big game hunting, but the sport is beginning to bore him. So he starts working out how he could get a certain dictator within range of his gun. And from being the pursuer he becomes the pursued. . . .

The first of innumerable sudden and mysterious deaths to occur in the detective genre: Arild Rosenkrantz's illustration for Poe's THE MURDERS IN THE RUE MORGUE, *a story in which there are two murders. In* THE MYSTERY OF MARIE ROGÊT *there is one, while in* THE PURLOINED LETTER *there are none. Even on this point Poe recognized the need for variety in his tales of the first detective in fiction.*

Right: John Buchan crowned his varied career as Governor-General of Canada. By then he had already written THE THIRTY-NINE STEPS, *filmed by Hitchcock with (right) Robert Donat and Madeleine Carroll.*

Even if Alfred Hitchcock never wrote a line himself he qualifies through his films as one of the great figures in the crime genre. Below: Cary Grant in NORTH BY NORTH-WEST *(MGM) (1959).*

Below: The TV series THE FUGITIVE *probably must hold the record for the longest flight — and chase — in history. From the left: David Janssen as the fugitive, Barry Morse as the public prosecutor, and Billy Raisch as the one-armed man, the real murderer.*

Clues

One of the ten commandments of detective writing drawn up by Father Ronald Knox is: *'The detective must not light on any clues which are not instantly produced for the inspection of the reader.'*

'Any writer can make a mystery by telling us that at this point the great Picklock Holes suddenly bent down and picked up from the ground an object which he refused to let his friend see. He whispers "Ha!" and his face grows grave – all that is illegitimate mystery-making. The skill of the detective author consists in being able to produce his clues and flourish them defiantly in our faces: "There!" he says, "What do you make of that?" and we make nothing.'

At one time the author would break off towards the end of a detective novel and say to his reader: 'All the facts of the case are in your possession; you should now be able to work for yourself who the murderer is!' – which, of course, we were quite unable to do without reading the author's explanation, when we would remark: 'Why, of course, who else could it be?'

These illustrations are examples of some of the clues that authors have given their readers. We all know the plan of the flat on Fifth Avenue or in Berkeley Square with X marking the spot where the corpse was found and the doors and windows so ingeniously sited that none of the suspects can be excluded. It is all fair play and delightfully scientific – as if we had in our hands one of the documents in the case. In the thirties Dennis Wheatley wrote a whole series of detective novels which were published in the form of facsimiles of documents, and included torn photographs, codes, typewritten reports, blood-stained pieces of clothing, railway tickets and the rest. They really did give the reader a chance of playing the detective.

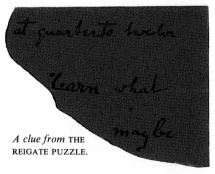

A clue from THE
REIGATE PUZZLE.

'The scene of the crime' as Conan Doyle
himself sketched it for THE NAVAL TREATY
(1894). One of the few spy stories he
wrote and, incidentally, an interesting
variation on 'the locked room' theme.

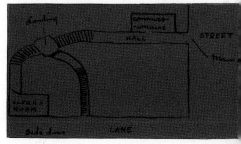

The identity of the guilty party has been discovered, now he has to be caught, and preferably alive. Illustration by Frederic Dorr Steele for Edward H. Hurlburt's LANAGAN, AMATEUR DETECTIVE *(1913).*

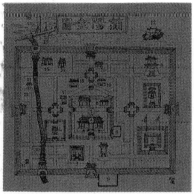

Nearly all Robert van Gulik's Magistrate Dee novels include detailed maps of temples, labyrinths, palaces or, as here, the entire town of Lan-fang, scene of THE CHINESE MAZE MURDERS *(1952), and* THE PHANTOM OF THE TEMPLE *(1966).*

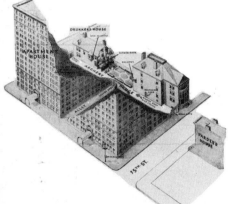

The scene of the murder in Van Dine's THE BISHOP MURDER CASE.

R. Austin Freeman's scientific detective, John Thorndyke, M.D., F.R.C.P., with his friend and assistant, Dr Christopher Jervis, investigates mysterious clues beneath a hansom cab. Illustration by H. M. Brock for the short story, THE ANTHROPOLOGIST AT LARGE, *in a collection of* JOHN THORNDYKE'S CASES *(1909), which contains various photomicrographs, plans, codes and ciphers.*

The spy story enters the field

Spy stories are said to go back to the Old Testament, when Moses sent spies into the Land of Canaan. But the first real spy novel, *The Riddle of the Sands*, dates from 1904 and was written by Erskine Childers. The story was anti-German and pro-British. But the extraordinary sequel is that Childers, the world's first secret agent writer, himself died before a firing squad at the hands of the British. He took part in the Irish Rebellion, was tried by court martial and shot. Since then his son has been a member of the Irish Government.

The first works of importance in the spy genre are: *The Secret Agent*, by the Polish exile, Joseph Conrad, whose work has a clear-cut anti-czarist tendency and who had first-hand experience of political underground activity; *The Thirty-Nine Steps* and other stories by John Buchan, all of them mixed up with power politics, with which Buchan was himself concerned; *Ashenden, or The British Agent* – brilliant short stories by Somerset Maugham and probably the best of the books in this list – and *The Three Couriers* by Compton Mackenzie, author of the novel on which the famous film, *Whisky Galore*, was based. These last writers both served in the British intelligence service.

'Count von Beilstein was a spy!' Sketch by T. Crawther for a novel by William le Queux, author of a long list of improbable political thrillers.

Above: Erskine Childers, author of THE RIDDLE OF THE SANDS, *a story set against the tension between Great Britain and Kaiser Wilhelm's Germany, thirsting for colonies and expanding its navy. The story starts in a yacht off the coast of South Jutland.*

Right: a rare picture of Mrs Childers during the gun-running which was one of the causes of her husband's execution.

A genre tailor-made for Hitchcock. In 1936 he filmed ASHENDEN, *with John Gielgud (background) in the title role, and Peter Lorre.*

Cover picture to THE THREE COURIERS. *Note the pockets bulging with revolvers.*

Below: the most famous agent of all: The Scarlet Pimpernel, from Baroness Orczy's novel. Left, in the title role, Leslie Howard; right, Raymond Massey.

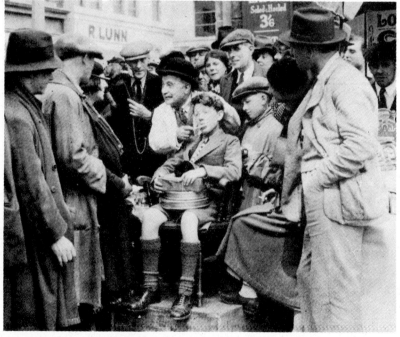

Hitchcock again: SABOTAGE, *based on Conrad's* THE SECRET AGENT, *with its anarchists and agents-provocateurs. A simple-minded boy is on his way through London with a time-bomb. He gets delayed . . . .*

'Black Mask', pioneer of the 'hard-boiled' style

'Black Mask' has its own niche in the history of crime writing – a pulp magazine that pioneered what has become known as the hard-boiled style. Hemingway was influenced by 'Black Mask'. Early in its career it had three writers who were mainly responsible for giving the American crime genre its characteristic features. These were Dashiell Hammett, Erle Stanley Gardner and Raymond Chandler. 'Black Mask' began the school of fast-moving events in a corrupt world. It launched the hard-hitting, quick-on-the-draw private detective. It developed the clipped style: 'He died leaving 10,000 in life insurance, no children, and a wife who hated him.'

WESTERN, DETECTIVE & ADVENTURE STORIES

BLACK MASK

JUNE 1929 · 20
IN CANADA 25c

Race Williams Never Bluffs

Below: Erle Stanley Gardner's earliest contributions to 'Black Mask' were wild-west stories.

Scum of the Border

By ERLE STANLEY GARDNER

Bob Larkin walks into trouble.

Typical 'Black Mask' cover, reproduced from a rare catalogue of the sensational exhibition, 'The Boys in the Black Mask', arranged in Los Angeles in 1961 by the University of California Library.

THE THIN MAN *may not be one of Hammett's best books but it was his biggest success, especially as a film: a witty burlesque, full of amusing lines. Below: Myrna Loy and William Powell.*

The US of gangsters and corruption

Dashiell Hammett is one of the great artists of crime writing. His material comes from the expert knowledge of the underworld, of the law, and of the corruption in the US that he acquired while working for Pinkerton's Detective Bureau. Those experiences gave him a rebellious attitude towards society. As a result he fell a victim to McCarthy's committee for unAmerican activities and his life ended in tragedy.

His main works were his short stories, most of which feature 'The Continental Op', the professional from the Continental Detective Bureau; *The Maltese Falcon* with Sam Spade, the prototype of all hard-boiled detectives, as the main figure; and *The Glass Key*, with intelligent Ned Beaumont, the expert at uncovering political swindles, as the mainspring of events.

Above: two characteristic types from THE GLASS KEY *(Paramount).*
Left: the principal characters in THE MALTESE FALCON, *played by (from the right) Sidney Greenstreet, Mary Astor and Peter Lorre, with Humphrey Bogart as the detective, Sam Spade (Warner Bros – First National Picture).*

The Quaker and oil careerist who became a great detective writer

Raymond Chandler was born in Chicago in 1888, the child of Quakers, and Quaker idealism permeates the outlook of his detective, Philip Marlowe. When his parents separated he accompanied his mother to England, the land of her birth, went to school there, became a literary critic (hence Philip Marlowe's literary interests), and fought in the First World War (hence the death and violence in his books). He returned to the US and made a career in the oil industry (hence his knowledge of the American business world). During the depression of 1929 he lost his job and created his detective, Philip Marlowe, a joyless man finding solace in whisky. The seven novels in which he appeared are all worth reading. Chandler was an alcoholic and died in 1959.

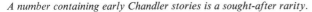

A number containing early Chandler stories is a sought-after rarity.

Left: Chandler during the First World War. Right: Chandler with his film director Billy Wilder. Jointly they were responsible for DOUBLE INDEMNITY, a star-studded film which Chandler felt rather proud of, although 'it shortened my life by several years'.

Fred MacMurray and Edward G. Robinson in DOUBLE INDEMNITY. Chandler wrote many other film scripts. In his novel THE LITTLE SISTER he took his revenge on Hollywood for all that he had suffered there. A film magnate in the novel sighingly refers to his company as 'the brothel', while gangsters in the wings engage in drug peddling and blackmail.

'She had a cast-iron smile . . .'

636-61

Chandler's individuality as an artist depends in part on his extremely personal style of writing. In one of his books the multi-millionaire's chauffeur spends his spare time studying literary history at the university. One of Chandler's characters says of him: 'I offered him a dollar tip but he wouldn't take it. I offered to buy him T. S. Eliot's poems. He said he had them already.' And of a cloakroom attendant in a night club he writes: 'She had a cast-iron smile and a pair of eyes that could count the money in the wallet you had in your back pocket.'

Los Angeles and Hollywood provided the scene for all Raymond Chandler's plots. His attitude to the film world was ambivalent. At one moment he would boast of having created with DOUBLE INDEMNITY (below) 'the high budget mystery picture trends'. The next moment his gall would flow. And yet with Humphrey Bogart as Philip Marlowe in THE BIG SLEEP Hollywood produced one of the great detective pictures (the two stills opposite). Dick Powell played Marlowe in the film version of FAREWELL, MY LOVELY (right, blindfolded).

Americans at the time of transition

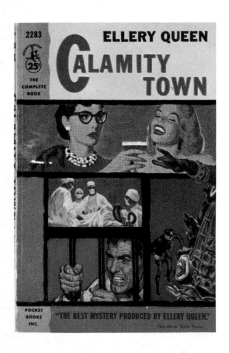

Mark Twain's PUDD'NHEAD WILSON began as the wildest of farces and ended by being one of his most trenchant and important novels.

CALAMITY TOWN (1942), the finest of Ellery Queen's more recent novels, is set in Wrightsville, an imaginary medium-sized town.

Mark Twain – Samuel L. Clemens – was greatly interested in crime and detective stories. In 1882 he published a wonderful parody, *The Stolen White Elephant*, followed by a tragedy, *Pudd'nhead Wilson*, which was the first novel to mention fingerprints. Two years later came *Tom Sawyer, Detective*; in 1902 *A Double Barrelled Detective Story*, a satire which had the misfortune to be taken seriously; and, after his death, the unfinished and unsuccessful tale, *Simon Wheeler, Detective*, which appeared in an annotated edition in 1963.

In the twenties there was a renaissance with the writings of S. S. Van Dine, a pseudonym concealing the New York journalist, Willard Huntington Wright (1888–1939). Van Dine's aristocratic millionaire detective, Philo Vance, is to some extent his creator's *alter ego*. Like Vance, Mr Wright appreciated exquisite food and elegant clothes; he was a painter, a bibliophile, and something of a poseur. His first novel, *The Benson Murder Case*, which appeared in 1926, was followed by eleven more, the last six of which are distinctly weaker than the first five. Ellery Queen, alias the cousins Frederic Dannay and Manfred B. Lee, made their début in 1929 with *The Roman Hat Mystery* which, like Van Dine's books was in the classic English style. But, whether as chronicler or detective, 'Ellery Queen' has undergone constant development, and today represents the quintessence of American detective story writing.

Since 1929 Frederic Dannay and Manfred B. Lee have written fifty books 'by', and about, the detective, Ellery Queen.

This violent scene from TOM SAWYER, DETECTIVE, *depicted by A. B. Frost, might have come from St. St. Blicher's story,* THE VICAR OF VEJLBYE (*Præsten i Vejlbye*).

Many of S. S. Van Dine's novels were based on contemporary cases of murder to some extent disguised. Several of them were filmed with William Powell in the role of the gentleman detective, Philo Vance, seen here with Edward Arnold in THE KENNEL MURDER CASE.

The religious detective

America's religious detective, Uncle Abner, first appeared about the same time as Father Brown in England. He, too, was in a number of short stories, most of which are excellent. Abner was the creation of Melville Davisson Post (1871–1930), a *grand seigneur* from West Virginia, the scene of the Abner stories. The first was *The Doomsdorf Mystery*. The period is the early nineteenth century. In a room locked on the inside Abner finds the body of the proprietor of an illicit drink shop. He has been shot with a revolver which is also in the room. Two persons outside confess to the murder, and Abner's Dr Watson, magistrate Randolph, believes them. But there is a surprising explanation to the mystery, with pointed allusions to the justice of God. The illustration from 'The Saturday Evening Post' below shows Uncle Abner accompanied by the magistrate with the self-accusing mistress of the dead man. Post wrote eighteen Abner stories, all of which are chronicled by Abner's nephew.

*Far left: the mark of a Post book (*THE BRADMOOR MURDER*), its hero a Scotland Yard detective. Far right: Collier Books' excellent modern edition of the Abner stories.*

Above, and bottom right: Melville Davisson Post in person.

Here is a characteristic anecdote about Abner. In his pocket he always carried a bible, which he would read whenever and wherever he felt inclined. Once as he sat reading it by the stove, the men in Roy's bar tried to poke fun at him – something they never tried again. When the fight was over Abner paid Roy eighteen silver dollars for the damage – and he was the only man in the bar able to ride home. 'My uncle belonged to the church militant, and his God was a war-god,' says the young nephew who recounts the incident. In one of the stories he is himself the victim of a dramatic attempt to murder him.

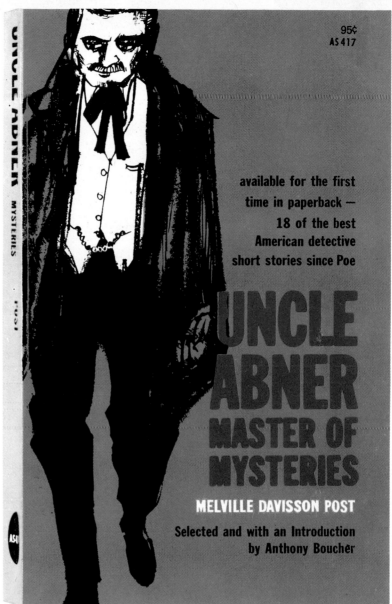

95¢
AS 417

available for the first time in paperback –
18 of the best American detective short stories since Poe

UNCLE ABNER MASTER OF MYSTERIES

MELVILLE DAVISSON POST

Selected and with an Introduction by Anthony Boucher

Post is an excellent writer, telling his tales with natural authority and masterly technique.

Nevertheless Post probably made his greatest contribution to the genre by inspiring William Faulkner, the Nobel Prizewinner, to write a collection of crime stories, *Knight's Gambit*, whose detective, Uncle Gavin, is modelled on Abner. Faulkner composes variations on themes by Post, giving them richer texture, more vivid orchestration, the touch of a supreme artist.

But his detective has the same trick of playing a practical joke to get the murderer to betray himself. As so often with Faulkner, the characters include the unfortunates of society: deaf mutes, orphans, the persecuted, and a mentally handicapped boy sentenced for two murders he did not commit.

Lawyer detectives

Arthur Train's sagacious
Mr Ephraim Tutt.

Lawyer detectives and crime stories based on trial scenes have long been popular. The first lawyer detective appeared as early as 1852 in Warren Warner's *The Experiences of a Barrister*. Evidently the public liked the book, for it ran to four editions in Britain and the US, and in 1884 was re-titled *The Lawyer-Detective*. 1896 saw the publication of Herbert Lloyd's *A Lawyer's Secret* and Melville Davisson Post's *The Strange Schemes of Randolph Mason*. Mason was an unscrupulous lawyer not unlike the one in Arthur Train's *The Confessions of Artemus Quibble* (1911). Nine years later, however, Arthur Train created an entirely different type of character in lovable old Ephraim Tutt with his inevitable cigar. Tutt uses his legal knowledge, without any thought of financial reward, to defend the helpless against rascally tycoons and swindlers. Harry Klingsberg's young

and idealistic district attorney and amateur astronomer, *John Doowinkle* (1940), is an equally attractive character, who frequently works in conjunction with his wife.

Ephraim Tutt and John Doowinkle are worthy colleagues of Erle Stanley Gardner's legendary Perry Mason, who made his début in *The Case of the Velvet Claws* and has since appeared in some 100 cases. His confidential secretary, Della Street, serves her chief with such devotion that one lives in the constant hope of a marriage between them.

Gardner has two other lawyer heroes: Doug Selby, district attorney of California, who made his début in *The D.A. Calls It Murder* in 1937; and Donald Lamb, an ex-lawyer who appears in the Gardner books published under the pseudonym of A. A. Fair, and who works with a mannish female colleague, Bertha Cool.

Erle Stanley Gardner, here seen as a young man, and at the peak of his writing career, is an extremely clever lawyer who, despite his productivity, has time to interest himself in real criminal cases. Together with other specialists in the field he has formed what he calls 'The Court of Last Resort', which takes up dubious judgments for further scrutiny and has helped a number of people in distress.

A magnificent example of a trial scene
from the film of Agatha Christie's novel,
WITNESS FOR THE PROSECUTION. *With
Tyrone Power as Leonard Vole,
Marlene Dietrich as his wife and, in
particular, Charles Laughton as Sir
Wilfrid Robarts, K.C., the film was an
immense success.*

An endless TV series with Raymond Burr
as Perry Mason did little to add to the
popularity of the novels, which could
hardly have been greater. But it is doubtful
whether Edward S. Aaron's novel about
Preston and Son, played on TV by E. G.
Marshall and Robert Reed, would be
remembered today if millions of viewers
had not followed their somewhat corny
battles for justice on the screen – though
it must be conceded thay they did not
hesitate to bring some ticklish subjects out
into the open.

The detective's first question: What was in the victim's will?

These two pictures illustrate the only crime novel written by Rider Haggard, the famous author of *King Solomon's Mines*. Its title, *Mr Meeson's Will* (1888), leads to the heart of a favourite theme in the genre: the will, and all that is thereby involved. Who stands to benefit by the victim's last will and testament? It is almost the first question the detective in charge of the case asks. A classic example of a 'last will and testament' novel full of lawyers, at least two of whom claim to be principal beneficiaries, is John Dickson Carr's *The Crooked Hinge*. But it contains a host of other incidents too. So does Rider Haggard's book. But the main plot concerns a successful woman novelist who, together with an angry publisher, the son of the Governor of New Zealand, and two seamen, gets stranded on a desert island. Angry publisher regrets he has disinherited attractive nephew, but no writing materials exist on island. A fresh will is *tattooed on the back* of the lovely novelist. All perish except the novelist and the child. This leads to the climax: the great battle in court. Is the will valid? The book belongs to the subsection known as the 'legal novel', which many authors have skilfully used as a means of attacking the judicial system. Examples are Raymond Postgate *(Verdict of Twelve)*, Edward Grierson (*Reputation for a Song*), Edgar Lustgarten (*A Case to Answer*), and the excellent Cyril Hare with his revelations of courts and lawyers (his best: *Tragedy at Law*).

The locked room and other trickology

Trickology is concerned with the tricks that writers use in their plots. This learned science traces an idea back to its originator – frequently Poe.

But there is an almost unknown originator in the field who deserves mention: Israel Zangwill. Zangwill wrote one book only in the genre before turning to other, less worthy, literary activities. The excellent book in question, *The Big Bow Mystery* (1891), is notable in that for the very first time in fiction a member of the police is implicated in the crime. A former head of the London police, retired and suffering from megalomania, meditates over the perfect crime that will baffle his successor . . . .

He commits a murder in a room which seems quite definitely to have been locked and inaccessible at the time of the murder. Here, too, Poe, and, for that matter, Gaboriau also, had forestalled him. But Zangwill was the first to construct a complete and wholly mystifying plot out of a problem which John Dickson Carr, among others, was later to handle so deftly in, for example, *The Red Widow Murders*, *The Judas Window* and *The Hollow Men*.

Mysterious code writing from R. Austin Freeman. Poe started it . . .

This drawing by an unknown artist illustrates the first instance of shadowing in world literature. The bearded young man is from Poe's short story, MAN OF THE CROWD. Full of detective curiosity he follows a man he imagines to be a criminal through the streets of London. In Poe's non-detective writings Ellery Queen claims to have found examples of fifteen or sixteen elements that recur in the genre. There would seem to be something in this. THOU ART THE MAN! contains (1) a person wrongly suspected; (2) an anonymous first-person chronicler, as subsequently employed by Hammett, for example; (3) false clues laid by the murderer; and (4) a murderer who is the least suspected person.

*Right: drawing by Arild Rosenkrantz
(brother of the crime writer, Palle Rosenkrantz) for Poe's* THOU ART THE MAN!
The least likely person proves to be guilty.

*Israel Zangwill was the first writer to put a
living personality into his book – no less a
person, in fact, than Mr Gladstone, the
Prime Minister.*

*Technology – shown in this drawing by
W. Clinton Pettee for an early spy story –
invades the detective's world as rapidly as
science affects police and secret service
methods. The logically deductive
detective finds life increasingly difficult.*

What tricks in crime writing was Poe *not* responsible for? Well, one is the trick of advancing the time of the murder to confuse the work of detection, as in *Trent's Last Case*. A more recent idea is the unexpected twist or, even better, *double* twist, at the end. Here, Carr, for example, is masterly. In the closing lines of one of his novels we learn that the delightful spinster who is its chief character is married. No sooner have we recovered from this shock than we hear that she will soon be a widow. 'How so?' 'Because her husband will be hanged for the murder!'

More Britons

Graham Greene has made a point of keeping his 'entertainments' distinct from the rest of his literary output, although it is sometimes difficult to see why, for example, *A Gun for Sale* could not equally well be placed in the serious section alongside *Brighton Rock* (1938), which is regarded by most critics as his best crime novel. The film classic, *The Third Man*, was originally written as a film script, and it was only after 'innumerable requests' that Greene decided in 1950 to base a book on the story and have it published together with *The Fallen Idol*. Other excellent 'entertainments' by Greene include *Stamboul Train* and *The Confidential Agent*.

One of the most interesting of modern English detective story writers is Julian Symons. After the publication of his first novel, *The Immaterial Murder Case*, in 1945, he gave careful thought to the potentialities of the crime story as serious literature. As a result he rejected the idea of there being any connection between the two. Like Nicholas Blake, he realized the absurdity of an author who dissects crime being bound by conventions and having to falsify reality. 'But the detective story can have an important artistic content,' says Julian Symons, and most of his books bear this view out.

Julian Symons as seen in 1938 by Wyndham Lewis.

Margery Allingham leaves the Paris police headquarters under the eye of a gendarme.

Scene from the film of Graham Greene's BRIGHTON ROCK. *The journalist, Fred Hale (Alan Wheatley), sees the gangsters approaching in a mirror.*

Roy Vickers
as a safe-breaker.
Caricature by
'Rich'.

*Margery Allingham (1904–66)
belonged to the intelligentsia of
crime writers. Her detective,
Albert Campion, improved in each
successive book she wrote, whether
he was fraternizing with artists or
hobnobbing in the exclusive circles
of Mayfair.*

*Roy Vickers (1888–1965) was
noted for his six collections of
short stories as the 'Department of
Dead-End Stories'. They were the
best examples of the 'inverted'
detective story since R. Austin
Freeman.*

*Nicholas Blake, photographed
right by Irving Penn, is the
pseudonym of Cecil Day Lewis
who, in addition to being poet
laureate, is Britain's first masculine crime writer of importance
since Crofts. Fine examples of his
work include* THE BEAST MUST
DIE *and* MINUTE FOR MURDER.

The strip cartoon detective

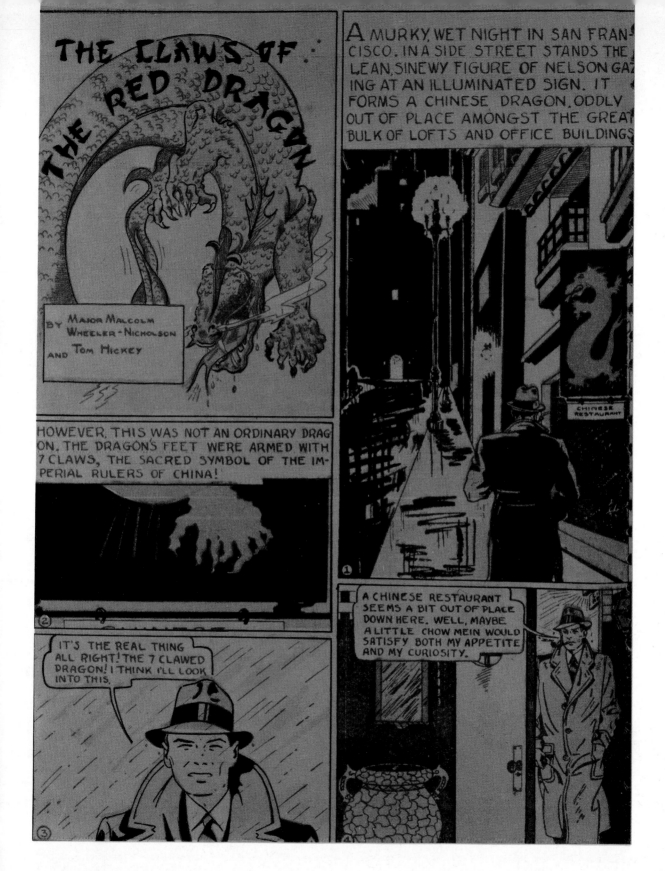

'A great event in strip cartoon history,' said Jules Feiffer, the great satirist who uses the comic strip as his medium, when 'Detective Comics' was launched in 1937. It was the first comic to be devoted entirely to detectives.

The rest of the world

Outside the US, Britain and France, most crime and detective novels have only succeeded in their country of origin. Few have achieved international fame. Disregarding the fact that Georges Simenon is Belgian by birth we find that Howard Haycraft and Ellery Queen name only the following from the rest of the world in their definitive list of the 'cornerstones' of the genre: the Austrian writer, Balduin Groller, whose tales of his detective, Dagobert Trostler, were published in Leipzig in 1910–12 and are now enjoying a revival as period pieces; Dostoievsky, whose *Rodion Raskolnikov* could with a little goodwill be called a crime novel; and the New Zealander, Ngaio Marsh. The Australian writer, Arthur W. Upfield, is not mentioned. Queen's list of the 106 most important collections of detective short stories includes the Argentinean, H. Bustos Domecq *(Six Problems for Isidro Parodi* – Seis problemas para Don Isidro Parodi – from 1942), and the Mexican writer, Antonio Helus *(The Duty to Murder* – La obligación de asesinar – from 1946); but many more might be added, e. g. the German writer, Paul Rosenhayn, whose detective, Joe Jenkins, was very popular in the twenties, even in the English speaking countries, where Karel Capek's two collections of short stories, *Tales from One Pocket* and *Tales from the Other Pocket*, are highly regarded.

The Argentinean writer, Jorge Luis Borges, has written some unusual psychological crime stories. They can be found in two of his short story collections, FICCIONES and LABYRINTHS (both 1962).

DETEKTIV DAGOBERTS TATEN UND ABENTEUER *(1910–12), by the Austrian writer, Balduin Groller, was republished in 1967.*

Balduin Groller's Dagobert Trostler, the 'Viennese Sherlock Holmes', and Joe Jenkins, the detective created by the German writer, Paul Rosenhayn, both achieved near international fame. Above: the cover of the first edition of DER FALL POMPEJUS PYM (1929), which contains facsimiles of the documents in the case.

Sketch by the Czech artist,
Vlastimil Rada, for Karel Čapek's
ironical story, SAFE-ROBBER AND
INCENDIARY, from the Austrian collection, DER GESTOHLENE KAKTUS (1937).

The first Russian crime novel in the USSR created something of a sensation in 1945. Entitled PETROVSKA 38, *phone number of the Moscow police headquarters, and written by Julian Semynov, it was immediately translated into ten languages.*

James Stewart in Hitchcock's film, VERTIGO, *based on the novel* D'ENTRE LES MORTS *by the French writers, Boileau and Narcejacs.*

Denmark, Norway —

At the beginning of the century Denmark was a trend-setter in crime writing. Palle Rosenkrantz (1867–1941) may not have been the first Scandinavian to write detective novels, but some of his work is among the best and most original in the genre. 1901 saw the publication of his *Retsbetjente*, the following year *Mordet i Vestermarie*, and 1903 *Hvad skovsøen gemte*. This was followed by thirteen other novels and collections of short stories.

Another writer with the versatility of Baron Rosenkrantz was Otto Rung (1874–1945). From 1908 onwards he wrote some 100 novels, among which his penetrating psychological and often humorous portraits of rascally Copenhageners are unsurpassed.

Drawing by Arne Ungermann for Tom Kristensen's MURDER IN THE PANTOMIME THEATRE *(Mord I Pantomimeteatret) (1962).*

Palle Rosenkrantz's AMTSDOMMER STERNER *(1906)*

– and Arild Rosenkrantz's cover to BARBERKNIVEN *(1907).*

Stein Riverton (Sven Elvestad) making notes in the Norwegian mountains for a crime story. Sketch by his friend, the Danish artist, Hans Bendix.

Crime fiction prize awarded by the Swedish tabloid, 'Expressen' – a 'Sherlock'.

Johannes V. Jensen's *Madame D'Ora* (1904), proves on closer examination to be a detective novel. But curiously enough the five languages into which it has been translated do not include English, although the action takes place in the US. Herman Jensen produced his first novel, *Den natlige gæst*, in 1918, after serving as a police officer first in the Cape and then in London's Chinese quarter. It is the first of a number of melodramatic books featuring the attractive figure of Rudolph Black as the detective. Next on the list is Jens Anker, alias Robert Hansen (1883–1957) with an equally appealing amateur detective, Arne Falk, who has been involved in twenty-seven mysteries. Among more recent Danish crime writers are Carlo Andersen, who won a Scandinavian prize in 1939 with *Krigstestamentet*, and Pierre Andrezel (Karen Blixen) with the classic thriller *The Angelic Avengers* (1944) (Gengaeldeelsens veje), while the most popular contemporary writers include Else Fischer, Peter Sander, Mogens Mugge Hansen, Bent Thorndahl, H. P. Jacobsen, Helle Stangerup and Anders Bodelsen (*Think of a Number*, 1969).

The two big names in Norwegian crime fiction, Øvre Richter Frich (1872–1945) and Stein Riverton (1884–1934), published their first books before the First World War. While Frich concentrated on crime in the style of Rocambole, the honour of creating the Norwegian detective novel belongs to Stein Riverton who, under his real name, Sven Elvestad, is a much respected figure in Scandinavian literature. His detective, Asbjørn Krag, is a typical Norwegian derivative of Sherlock Holmes. Many of his novels are still worth reading, e.g. *Jernvognen* and *Manden som ville plyndre Kristiania*. The latest writers include Gerd Nyquist, Helge Hagerup and Michael Grundt Spang.

– and Sweden

The first Swedish detective story mentioned in Jörgen Elgström and Åke Runnquist's *The Swedish Book of Murder* (Svensk mordbok) is by Prins Pierre, pseudonym of Fredrik Lindholm, whose *Stockholms-detektiven* of 1898 is now only of historic interest. For years Sweden's leading author in the field was Frank Heller (1886–1947), alias Dr Gunnar Serner of Lund. His most famous character, Filip Collin, was a gentleman crook. An English translation, *The London Adventures of Mr Collin*, was published in 1924. Heller's masterpiece, *Kejsarens gamla kläder* (1918), is a Danish-Swedish-Chinese intrigue laid in Copenhagen, while his Dr Zimmertür stories also deserve mention.

Maria Lang, alias Dagmar Lang, one of the big names in Swedish crime fiction ever since her début in 1949. Several of her books have been translated into English. Top: scene from the film of her book, KUNG LILJEKONVALJE AV DUNGEN, *with Karl Arne Holmsten as the detective, Christer Wijk.*

Frank Heller's early books featured Filip Collin, a wily scholar from Lund, full of charm. Like all the best gentlemen crooks he was often on the side of the angels. The stories were illustrated by some of Sweden's best artists. Sketch by Yngve Berg from the first Filip Collin book.

Fourth in this quartet of Swedish masters is Hans Krister Rönblom, who died in 1964 (DÖD BLAND DE DÖDA, 1954, and TALA OM REP, 1958). Sweden still produces first-rate detective writers, among them Kerstin Ekman, whose breakthrough came in 1961 with DE TRE SMÅ MÄSTARNE, Jan Ekström (TRÄPRÄCKEN, 1963, and MORIANERNA, 1964) and the duo, Maj Sjöwall-Per Wahlöö.

Stieg Trenter, whose sudden death in 1967 shocked his many friends, seen in his beloved Florence.

Sune Lundquist, famous under his pseudonym, Vic Suneson, is among the most brilliant of Sweden's detective writers. Since 1948 he has written nineteen crime novels and two collections of short stories featuring Commissioner O. P. Nilsson.

The realistic police novel

The latest development in the crime story is represented by the 'procedural school' – the realistic novel describing the painstaking work carried out in laboratories, offices, and in the field by the police themselves. This type of story became immensely popular a few years ago, and there is no sign of its popularity waning, for the best exponents of the school know their subject and are first-rate writers. Outstanding examples are Maurice Procter, who served for twenty years in the Halifax police force before he began writing about Chief Inspector Marteneau; Ed McBain, alias Evan Hunter, whose Steve Carella of New York's 87th District is a familiar figure from numerous books and TV; and several from Scotland Yard, including J. J. Marric (John Creasey), with his very appealing George Gideon.

A scene from Sidney Kingsley's play, DETECTIVE STORY *(1949), revealing for first time the dreariness of the police station. The play was made into a book and also filmed, with Kirk Douglas as the complex-ridden policeman who takes it out on the big- and small-time criminals he encounters. Kingsley's milieu became the model for Ed McBain's classic Station 87, and does not greatly differ from the prosaic precincts of all big American towns, from Maigret's quarters on the Quai des Orfèvres, or from a police station in Amsterdam.*

The identification of criminals is an important element in the realistic police novel. This example is from John Huston's 1954 film of W. R. Burnett's famous gangster novel, THE ASPHALT JUNGLE, which had appeared five years previously.

The corpulent guardian of the law of 1895 has little in common with the policeman of today.

Leif Panduro's Danish TV series, DO YOU LIKE OYSTERS?, was a big Scandinavian success in 1967, but the police, played by Pouel Kern and Erik Paaske, were criticized for being unrealistic.

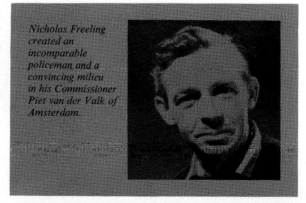

Nicholas Freeling created an incomparable policeman and a convincing milieu in his Commissioner Piet van der Valk of Amsterdam.

J. J. Marric's GIDEON'S DAY (1955), launched George Gideon of Scotland Yard. Under his real name, John Creasey, Marric has also written a long series featuring Inspector Roger West, another product of the realistic school.

Murder for fun

'May I take the message?
Her Ladyship has just curled up
with Peter Cheyney.' Drawing
from 1947 by Tom Cottrell
('S. Seymour').

John Creasey's numerous crime anthologies, published under the general title, JOHN CREASEY'S MYSTERY BEDSIDE BOOKS, *are enlivened by humorous drawings. This picture without words appears at the end of Volume I (1960).*

Crime is not normally a source of fun, but crime fiction includes a large number of light-hearted parodies and pastiches. This drawing by Gluyas Williams is from Corey Ford's THE ROLLO BOYS WITH SHERLOCK HOLMES *(1925), a book which also pokes fun at Michael Arlen's high society novels.*

The American humorist, John Kendrick Bangs, is almost forgotten now, though he was extremely popular at the turn of the century. Bangs was very fond of putting well-known literary characters in new situations. Sherlock Holmes, for instance, frequently appears in his descriptions of Parnassus and Hades.
In MRS RAFFLES (1905) – illustrated by Albert Levering – 'Bunny' Manders recounts the adventure of 'an amateur crackswoman' who is described as the widow of A. J. Raffles.

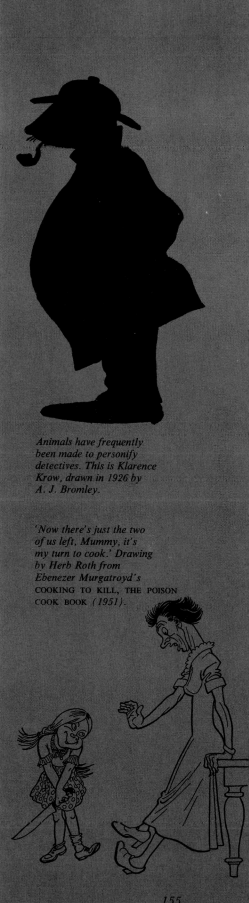

Animals have frequently been made to personify detectives. This is Klarence Krow, drawn in 1926 by A. J. Bromley.

'Now there's just the two of us left, Mummy, it's my turn to cook.' Drawing by Herb Roth from Ebenezer Murgatroyd's COOKING TO KILL, THE POISON COOK BOOK (1951).

More humour

As a great admirer of Holmes, the Danish humorist Robert Storm Petersen founded the first Sherlock Holmes society in Denmark. He also wrote and illustrated a number of delightful parodies featuring Holm and Madsen (above). Storm-P. shared Holmes's and Conan Doyle's love of good shag tobacco, as witness his book EN PIBE TOBAK (1933).

The American strip-tease artist, Gypsy Rose Lee, sketched at her typewriter by Vertès. Her detective novel, THE G-STRING MURDERS (1941), was a tour de force, though the milieu was unfamiliar to her fellow writers. Her second attempt in the genre was less successful.

Carl Muusmann wrote a pastiche in 1906 entitled SHERLOCK HOLMES AT MARIENLYST (Sherlock Holmes på Marienlyst). This illustration of Holmes in an embarrassing situation is by Carsten Ravn.

'I shot him with a bow and arrow because I didn't want to wake the children.' Drawing by Paton from one of John Creasey's anthologies.

Petty criminals forgathering in a Copenhagen tavern – an impression by Aage Borresø for C. Cherly's MYSTERIES FROM COPENHAGEN, OR THE GRØNNEGADE PRINCESS *(Kobenhavns mysterier, eller Prinsessen fra Grønnegade).*

'This is too good to be true!' Drawing by Hudson. Alongside: cover drawing by Tom Walker for THE SCIENCE-FICTIONAL SHERLOCK HOLMES, *published by the US Sherlock Holmes society, 'The Council of Four' in 1960 and containing pieces about the detective stretching far into the future.*

The spy returns – and stays

Stimulated by the unrest and upheavals in Europe prior to the Second World War, the 'political thriller', the spy, or special agent novel enjoyed a revival in the thirties. Today the genre is still the most popular in the western world. It is symptomatic of the world we live in that the detective has had to yield pride of place to the secret agent.

One of the first in the field was Graham Greene, whose most important early works deal with insignificant, inhibited, ordinary people who get caught in the web of world politics. In *Stamboul Train* a political emigré leaves his teaching job at a dull boarding-school to start a revolution, but it all ends in disaster. In *A Gun for Sale* the villain is the armament industry, which sends a young gangster with a hare-lip out to murder the foreign minister of a European state. In *The Confidential Agent*, with its portrait of a self-tormenting lecturer in Romance languages who knows prisons and party intrigues from the inside, the action is set against the background of the Spanish Civil War. In *The Ministry of Fear* the milieu is the London of the blitz, with a wife-murderer who gets unwillingly involved with the fifth-column.

Greene is a master at making the spy novel a chronicle of his times, with the solitary individual confronted by the menace of power politics.

Below: Alan Ladd as the hired political assassin in the Paramount film of Graham Greene's A GUN FOR SALE *(directed by Frank Tuttle). The gunman, hunted by the police, is himself hunting down his employer who has paid him in forged notes.*

A name to set beside Graham Greene in the renaissance of the spy genre is also an Englishman, Eric Ambler (right). His political attitude reflects the fluctuating and uncertain reactions of the democratic world to the varying political movements of recent decades: neutralism, anti-fascism, pro-popular front, anti-big industrialism, pro-Soviet, anti-Stalinist. With John le Carré he is the most exciting and committed of special agent writers. Two other first-class books are: DRINK TO YESTERDAY by Manning Coles, with its theme of the loneliness of the spy, and THE CASE OF THE JOURNEYING BOY by Michael Innes; this, with a boy as the main character, tends to lay the emphasis on adventure and humour.

A border incident occurs between two Balkan countries. According to the telegram reports soldiers in one country have fired on some peasants in the other. State No. 2 decides to strengthen its defences with new anti-aircraft guns. The guns are supplied by a Belgian factory and the deal is financed by the Eurasian Credit Trust. Later, State No. 1 reports that those firing the shots were not soldiers but professional terrorists. They were paid to stage the incident by a man of whom they know nothing except that he came from Paris. Just such a man is Dimitrios, the central figure in Ambler's main work, THE MASK OF DIMITRIOS. An English university lecturer in political science – an expert in national socialism and spare time writer of escapist detective stories – traces Dimitrios's career through a network of international crimes ranging from drug smuggling, white slave trafficking, prostitution and political terrorism to large-scale trading with governments in arms. Dimitrios is not wicked. Good business or bad is the basis of his theology. The situation is typical in Ambler's writing: the civilized, uncommitted, slightly naive Englishman confronted by the efficient and effective cynicism of the modern world. But there is no need to fear that this brief summary will in any way diminish the excitement of the book. Ambler is a master at conveying a sense of excitement and peril.

THE MASK OF DIMITRIOS
ERIC AMBLER

One more story like EPITAPH FOR A SPY and CAUSE FOR ALARM and I shall have to say that Mr. Eric Ambler is easily the best living writer of thrillers
Philip Hewitt-Myring in News Chronicle

Commander Ian Fleming

When Ian Fleming published his thriller of high stakes and international intrigue, *Casino Royale,* in 1953, no critic predicted world-wide fame for him and his Agent 007. Nor was the success of the next three stories, *Live and Let Die, Moonraker* and *Diamonds Are Forever*, in any way sensational, although Raymond Chandler had written that Fleming was probably the most important writer of 'what are still, presumably, called *thrillers* in England'. It was only in 1957, with *From Russia with Love*, that Ian Fleming's breakthrough occurred with a boom that resounded throughout the world. Heads of state and leading intellectuals then declared that James Bond was their favourite reading. And when the films began to appear book sales rocketed.

To most James Bond fans the Scottish actor, Sean Connery, is the very incarnation of Agent 007. This still from the film version of FROM RUSSIA WITH LOVE *shows him in a typical situation. Like* THUNDER-BALL, *the film was directed by Terence Young.*

James Bond's knowledge of firearms is formidable and he always gets his man even if, as here, he has to use telescopic sights.

Ian Fleming, painted by Amherst Villiers. The picture is reproduced in colour as the frontis-piece to a de luxe edition limited to 250 signed copies of ON HER MAJESTY'S SECRET SERVICE *(1963). Ian Lancaster Fleming was born in 1908 and educated at Eton and Sandhurst. During the war he was secretary to the head of naval intelligence and when, as Commander Ian Fleming, R.N.V.R., he was demobilized in November 1945, he was a man without roots. He had frequently talked of settling in Jamaica, where he would write books and lie in the sun. The dream came true the following year, when he built an idyllic villa, 'Goldeney', near the little banana port of Orcabassa. After marrying Lady Anne Rothermere, who was divorced on his account and became the only woman in his life, Fleming used to overwinter each year in Jamaica and write Bond books. He died on 12 August 1964 after a heart attack. More than forty million copies of his books have been sold.*

Ian Fleming's only decoration was a Danish one – Commander of the Order of the Dannebrog – and that, he said, he got by chance.

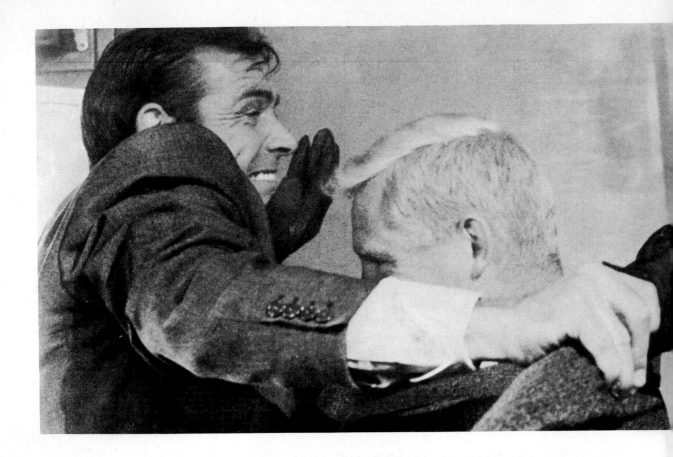

James Bond lives at least twice

For a pithy description of James Bond we need only turn to the card-index of the SMERSH organization, where we read:

First name: James. Height: 183 centimetres; weight: 76 kilograms; slim build; eyes: blue; hair: black; scar down right cheek and left shoulder; signs of plastic surgery on back of right hand; all-round athlete; expert pistol shot, boxer, knife-thrower; does not use disguises. Languages: French and German. Smokes heavily (N.B.: special cigarettes with three gold bands); vices: drink, but not to excess, and women . . .

Lovely girls are vital to James Bond if he is to develop his superman image to the full. Helping him to do just that is Ursula Andress in DR NO.

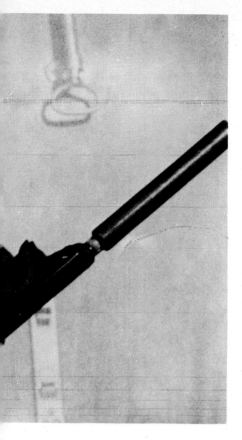

The bathroom scene in YOU ONLY LIVE TWICE *is an example of how the films gave the James Bond adventures a degree of irony certainly not intended by the author. The picture of Agent 007 as the saviour of world peace, as drawn in the books, becomes science fiction when presented in technicolour.*

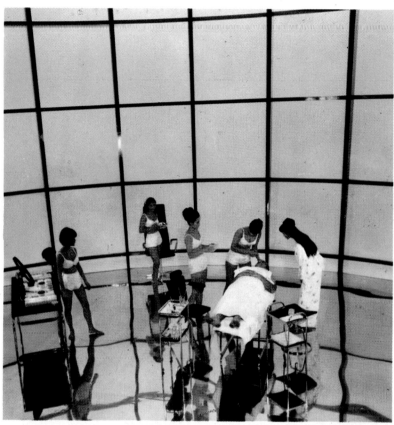

Ian Fleming was accused of exploiting sex and sadism. Whether this fight in FROM RUSSIA WITH LOVE *falls within the second category is for the reader to judge.*

James Bond could not of course be allowed to die with his author. The pseudonym Robert Markham conceals the name of Kingsley Amis, one of the most popular English authors of the fifties and among the first to write a James Bond biography. Now he has written COLONEL SUN, *a story in which Bond's chief, M, alias Admiral Sir Miles Messervy, gets kidnapped and carried off to a small Greek island, where sinister Colonel Lun Liang-tan, of the Chinese People's Liberation Army, re-sides. Bond comes to the rescue, accompanied by a charming Greek girl and her uncle, once a freedom fighter and now a conservative. The reader might easily imagine the book to be a posthumous work of Fleming's.*

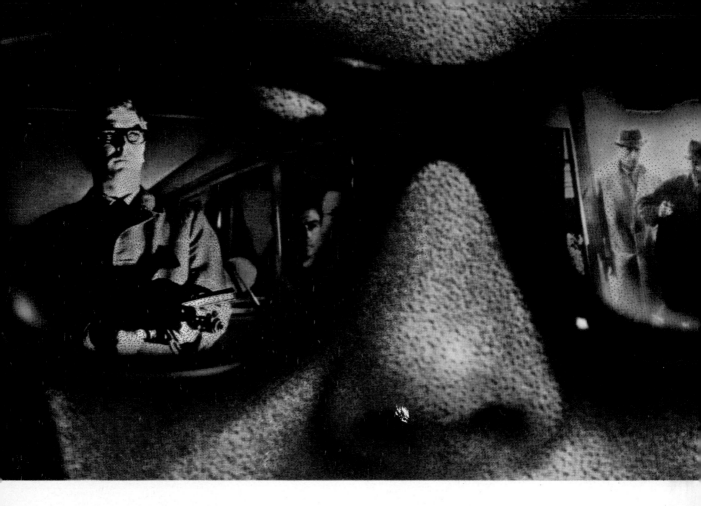

Not even their nearest and dearest dare they confide in . . . .

262393
24305

28/3/67   13 36

TO DIR OF INT
FROM SEC DEFENSE

77224   25334   87129   98910   44118
2556-   54-78   66115   91111   98321

262393   WASH

TO DIRECTOR OF INTELLIGENCE
FROM SECRETARY OF DEFENSE
ACTIVATE OPERATION EXPENSIVE
PLACE STOP LONDON IN
GO CONDITION

TOP SECRET

DATE   28/3/67
TIME   0800
DECODING OFFICER   APH.

TOP SECRET	
AUTHORIZATION TO TAKE COPIES	C.I.D.22
COPY NUMBER	5
DATE	28/3/67

At this point in the history of the spy genre one would need a computer and staff of experts to track the torrent of special agent books now flooding the international book market. The terrible reality behind this world of fiction is thrust upon us daily by the press and TV. After Fleming the most successful author in the genre is John le Carré (pseudonym of a former Eton master, David Cornwell). He debunks the repellent world of the special agent and writes of the bureaucrats and civil servants floundering behind the scenes, spurred by ambition and vanity and by traditions that time has outrun. He describes the loneliness of the spy, the slave of his own silence. Not even his nearest and dearest dare he confide in. The alien town surrounds him with a sinister atmosphere of Kafkaesque menace. What is he but a human being? He can die. And when he does, his colleagues go to his home to tell his widow. But all they find is a ten-year-old child. And then comes the farcical, revealing comment on all the official mumbo-jumbo of secrecy. *She* knows the mystery that surrounded her father. The irony of this grim vignette is characteristic of le Carré.

Another writer in the special agent field, in the John le Carré class, is also an Englishman: Len Deighton. His best book, THE IPCRESS FILE, was made into the most successful of the many spy films of the period. Michael Caine played the Bohemian gourmet who was the chief character. *Left and below: scenes from the film.*

Left: John le Carré, one of the finest writers in the spy genre after Graham Greene (from whom he learnt) and Eric Ambler. The picture was taken during the filming of his most famous work, THE SPY WHO CAME IN FROM THE COLD. Beside him is the director, Martin Ritt. The sales of this book surpass even those of Ian Fleming's. His two other books in the form are CALL FOR THE DEAD and THE LOOKING-GLASS WAR. Le Carré has also written a single crime novel, A MURDER OF QUALITY. All four books were extremely successful, although THE LOOKING-GLASS WAR was probably the best.

Driven to extremes

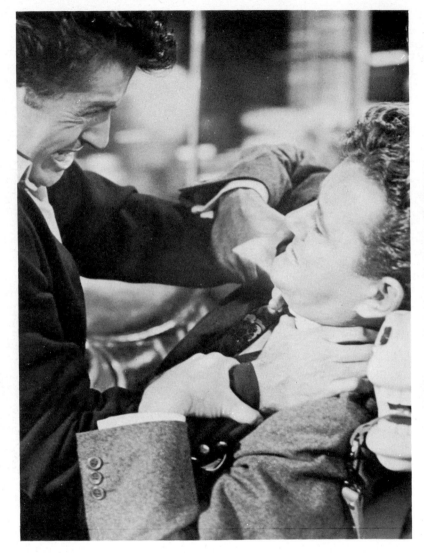

Left: Farley Granger and Robert Walker in Patricia Highsmith's STRANGERS ON A TRAIN, *directed by Hitchcock. The plot is that two murderers secretly exchange victims so that each murders a victim with whom he cannot be linked.*

The most distinctive and original crime writer today is Patricia Highsmith. Detectives clearing up crime are not in her line. The occasional policeman in her books is either a brutal third-degree interrogator or an anonymous blockhead. Her characters are people who would generally be regarded as normal but who have defects or tendencies within them that find an outlet, when they are driven to extremes, in violence, lunacy and murder.

Patricia Highsmith, an American by birth, skilfully describes the dark, hidden stresses behind the respectable facade of American society. Nowadays she lives in Europe – an emigrée from the land of her birth. Europeans and European milieux also figure in her books, all of which are eminently readable.

Above: Gert Froebe as the murderer in a French film version of THE BLUNDERER. *Right: Alain Delon, holding a Buddha statue, in the title role of* THE TALENTED MR RIPLEY. *Both these books were based on extremely original ideas. In the latter, the murderer goes free – at any rate for the time being. Patricia Highsmith has very little respect for the conventions.*

The brilliant cover picture for THE CRY OF
THE OWL *(Pan Books) – a typical
Highsmith novel. Its characters are the
types we have come to expect: a weak man,
a bungler, a voyeur – sympathetically
described and set against a psychopathic
bully; a sweet, infatuated girl contrasted
with a whore. The first two, in particular,
are recurring figures in Patricia Highsmith's books.*

*Patricia Highsmith, American by birth,
now living in Europe.*

Simenon
and
Maigret

In 1940 Georges Simenon wrote the following brief autobiography: 'Born in Liège, Belgium. At 16 was reporter in Liège for the "Gazette". At 17 published my first novel, *Au Pont des Arches*. Married at 20 and moved to Paris. Between the ages of 20 and 30 published about 200 escapist novels under 16 pseudonyms and sailed in a small yacht all round Europe. At 30 wrote my first detective novel on board my boat *Ostrogot* in Holland, creating Police Inspector Maigret. For two years wrote a Maigret novel a month. At 33 said farewell to crime fiction and could at last write more personal works. That is the whole story.

In fact it was not to be so. After 1940 Simenon did become one of the most important 'serious' writers in modern European literature, but his books often had a background of crime, and he did not abandon Maigret.

He goes on writing three to four novels a year in his house in Switzerland and has already published his 400th book. Maigret has become one of the greatest international successes in crime fiction, not only with the general public but also with the most fastidious of critics.

Simenon drawn by Vlaminck. Many important contemporary painters are members of Simenon's circle, and a first-rate novel of his, LE PETIT SAINT, *is about an artist.*

Arne Ungermann's sketch of Maigret, well armoured in his thick overcoat, interrogating one of Montmartre's 'filles de joie'. He's got the wrong coat on, of course. Paris weather is unpredictable, and as the morning draws on so does spring. Maigret sweats, feels unwell and longs for a glass of beer. No one can describe Paris in all weathers and seasons so well as Simenon. One should have a map beside one when reading him. Maigret does most of his investigating himself, so he knows Paris in detail: the boulevards (he himself lives on the Boulevard Richard-Lenoir), the murky district round the Place des Vosges where he also lived (in a flat borrowed from Simenon), the Seine quays, the regions bordering the canals, the parks . . . he visits them all, stopping at a bar now and then for a Calvados – the brandy made from Normandy apples.

An autobiographical sketch of Jules Maigret, police inspector in Paris, would be something like this: 'I was born in central France not far from Moulins. My father was a land agent, but though I wanted to be a doctor the fates decreed that I should be a policeman, working my way up through the ranks on my two feet and on my bicycle. There's no denying my marriage to Louise has been a happy one for I've written a book about it. Sherlock Holmes wrote learned papers. I've written memoirs *(Les Memoires de Maigret)*. It happened this way. One day at La Sûreté I received a visit from a journalist, Georges Sim, later known as Simenon. He was a lively chap and started writing books about me. All a bit exaggerated. Even after I'd retired he went on writing about my experiences. And he also hit on the idea of the memoirs. Much against my will he made me world famous. But I must admit he did it well.'

Maigret's sign: his hat and pipe, as drawn by the Swedish artist, Vidar Forsberg.

Maigret, again seen from behind, by the Swedish artist, Kjell Ivan Anderson. Simenon, too, made his back expressive. All that can be seen of the front of him is his faithful pipe. Maigret, has a far more natural attitude to his pipes than Holmes. He loves them as he loves his wife. Once after buying himself a pipe he was smitten with remorse and went into the next shop to send his wife a handkerchief embroidered with the arms of Lausanne. Typical Maigret.

Maigret in films and on TV

Apart from the Maigret books Simenon has written some of the finest psychological thrillers in crime fiction, the best of which is probably *The Man Who Watched the Trains Go By* (L'homme qui regardait passer les trains). It is the story of a petit bourgeois Dutchman driven, like a Patricia Highsmith character, to extremes. He leaves his wife and children, murders his chief's mistress, conceals himself with the greatest skill in Paris, brilliantly evades the police – and feels at last that he is alive. Only as a criminal can he become a real person, be free.... The detective engaged in hunting him down in Paris is Police Inspector Lucas of the Maigret books. Another example of a Simenon 'suspense novel' is the story of a mass murderer, *Les Fantômes du Chapelier*.

Harry Baur, the first and probably the finest Maigret. Baur succeeded in conveying the religious element in Maigret's make-up. As Professor Herbert Tingsten writes: 'Great detectives can serve as God or father symbols . . . and of all the great detectives Maigret is best fitted to fulfil the role. There is a melancholy integrity and efficiency in his actions which – to the religious minded – turn one's thoughts towards both an avenging and a forgiving God.'

Maigret's screen successes were followed by his TV successes. This picture shows Simenon, second from the left, with four TV Maigrets: the English, the German (Heinz Ruhmann), the Italian and, extreme right, the Dutch. The four had gathered to attend the unveiling of Pieter Dhondt's statue of Maigret in Delfzijl, Holland, where the first Maigret book was written. This was Simenon at the summit of success.

Jean Gabin as the detective in the film MAIGRET SETS A TRAP. *Gabin brought out the brutality in Maigret – the man who would not hesitate to slap a girl's face or knock a pornography dealer's tooth out.*

The man behind Maigret

In 1941, during the German occupation of France, Simenon wrote a book of memoirs, *Pedigree*. He wrote it because a doctor had told him he had only two years to live, and he wanted his children to know something of his childhood and youth. Anyone seeking deeper understanding of Maigret – the man who is constantly recalling his own childhood – could not do better than read this and other autobiographical works by Simenon.

Simenon at the age of three. His most harrowing descriptions of childhood appear in his novel IL PLEUT BERGERE.

Simenon's mother and father photographed in 1915 by their son, Georges, when he was twelve: she, strange and different to the point of mental disorder, he, calm, precise, and suffering from a weak heart. Their characteristics and milieu recur constantly in Simenon's books. The years in Liège have been a prime source of inspiration in Simenon's output.

Nine years old and very serious. Much of this world's malice, which he was later to describe, he experienced as a child in Liège.

A touching picture of Simenon blowing his nose in embarrassment after unveiling the statue of Maigret. Gradually he has become as famous as his character. He writes a novel in ten to twelve days between 6.30 and 2. During that time he is completely absorbed, 'en plein roman', alone with his paper and his pipes.

It is curious to see how, in later life, Simenon has adopted the big moustache of his father – the man whom he delineated so movingly in his autobiographical novel, PEDIGREE, and some of whose characteristics reappear in Maigret. Maigret is one of the few detectives in fiction who had a childhood! What sort of children would Sherlock Holmes, Sam Spade, and Philip Marlowe have been?

Bibliography

This list covers only the principal books, articles and magazines dealing with the subject. As regards the copious literature on Sherlock Holmes and Dr Watson the selection is particularly restricted, only essential works being mentioned. Those who would like to delve more deeply into the abundance of essays, articles and anthologies on the subject are referred, *inter alia*, to Howard Haycraft's *Murder for Pleasure* (American edition pp. 279–97), Fritz Wölken's *Der Literarische Mord* (pp. 321–40) and Jan Broberg's *Mord för ro skull* (pp. 261–6). A bibliography compiled by James G. Ollé (*The Literature on the Detective Story*), appeared in the July 1960 number of 'The Library World' (pp. 11–14). (List completed to June 1968.)

MARCEL ACHARD: *Sophocle et Archimède, pères du roman policier* (Liège 1960. 12 pp.)

KINGSLEY AMIS: *The James Bond Dossier* (London 1965. 159 pp.)

JENS AKER: *Kriminalromaner* (Copenhagen 1948. 126 pp.)

ROBERT ASHLEY: *Wilkie Collins* (London 1952. 144 pp.)

FELIX AYLMER: *The Drood Case* (London 1964. 228 pp.)

RICHARD M. BAKER: *The Drood Murder Case* (Berkeley, Calif. 1951. 207 pp.)

WILLIAM S. BARING-GOULD: *Nero Wolfe of West Thirty-fifth Street* (New York 1969. 203 pp.)

H. W. BELL (ed.): *Baker Street Studies* (London 1940. 344 pp.)

E. C. BENTLEY: *Those Days* (London 1940. 344 pp.)

TED BERGMAN: *Sherlock Holmes. A bibliography of the Swedish translations of Dr. John H. Watson's Sherlock Holmes stories I (1891-1916)* (Stockholm 1964. 39 pp.)

PIERRE BOILEAU & THOMAS NARCEJAC: *Le roman policier* (Paris 1964. 235 pp.)

MARY VICKHAM BOND: *How 007 Got His Name* (London 1966. 62 pp.)

ANTHONY BOUCHER: *Ellery Queen. A double profile* (Boston 1951. 12 pp.)

ANN S. BOYD: *The Devil with James Bond* (Richmond, Virginia 1966. 123 pp.)

THE BOYS IN THE BLACK MASK. *Catalogue from an exhibit in the University of California Library* (Los Angeles 1961. 12 pp.)

HERBERT BREAN (ed.): *The Mystery Writer's Handbook* (New York 1956. 268 pp.)

GAVIN BREND: *My Dear Holmes* (London 1951. 184 pp.)

DENNIS T. BRETT: *Crime Detection. A reader's guide* (Cambridge 1959. 350 pp.)

JAN BROBERG: *Mord för ro skull* (Malmö 1964. 303 pp.)

J. A. R. BROOKS: *Murder in Fact and Fiction* (London 1925. 282 pp.)

JOHN BUCHAN *by His Wife and Friends* (London 1947. 304 pp.)

ORESTE DEL BUONO & UMBERTO ECO (ed.): *The Bond Affair* (London 1966. 173 pp.)

A. S. BURACK (ed.): *Writing Detective and Mystery Fiction* (Boston 1945. 237 pp.)

ROGER CAILLOIS: *Le roman policier* (Buenos Aires 1941. 73 pp.)

CELESTINE PIERRE CAMBIAIRE: *The Influence of Edgar Allan Poe in France* (New York 1927. 322 pp.)

JOHN DICKSON CARR: *The Life of Sir Arthur Conan Doyle* (New York 1949. 305 pp.)

JOHN DICKSON CARR: *The Grandest Game in the World* (New York 1963. 22 pp.)

JOHN CARTER: *Collecting Detective Fiction* (London 1938. 63 pp.)

FRANK WADLEIGH CHANDLER: *The Literature of Roguery I-II* (Boston 1907. 584 pp.)

RAYMOND CHANDLER: *Raymond Chandler Speaking. Edited by Dorothy Gardiner & Kathrine Sorley Walker* (Boston 1962. 271 pp.)

G. K. CHESTERTON: *Autobiography* (London 1936. 348 pp.)

CHIMERA: *A Special issue on detective fiction. Vol. 5 (1947), no. 4* (New York 1947. 80 pp.)

PHILIP COLLINS: *Dickens and Crime* (London 1962. 371 pp.)

THE CRIME WRITER: *The journal of the Crime Writer's Association* (London 1954 –).

WALTER DAHNKE: *Kriminalroman und Wirklichkeit* (Hamburg 1958. 260 pp.)

NUEL PHARR DAVIS: *The Life of Wilkie Collins* (Urbana, Illinois 1956. 360 pp.)

PEER DEGN: *Blodige fotspor. Litt om eldre utenlandsk kriminallitteratur* (Oslo 1943. 19 pp)

FRIEDRICH DEPKEN: *Sherlock Holmes, Raffles und ihre Vorbiler* (Heidelberg 1914. 105 pp.)

AUGUST DERLETH: *Praed Street Papers* (New York 1965. 82 pp.)

DETECTIVE FICTION. *A collection of first and a few early editions* (Catalogue from The Schribner Bookstore. New York 1934. 79 pp.)

DETECTIVE FICTION (*Catalogue* from Charles Rare Books. Buntingford 1955. 25 pp.)

WALTER DEXTER: *Some Rogues and Vagabonds of Dickens* (London 1927. 284 pp.)

ADRIAN CONAN DOYLE: *The True Conan Doyle* (London 1945. 24 pp.)

ARTHUR CONAN DOYLE: *Memories and Adventures* (London 1924. 408 pp.)

PHILIP DURHAM: *Down These Mean Streets a Man Must Go, Raymond Chandler's Knight* (Durham, North Carolina 1963. 173 pp.)

JÖRGEN ELGSTRÖM, TAGE LA COUR & ÅKE RUNNIQUIST: *Mord i biblioteket* (Stockholm 1961. 223 pp. – Danish edition, Copenhagen 1965.)

JÖRGEN ELGSTRÖM & ÅKE RUNNIQUIST: *Svensk mordbok. Den svenska detektivromanens historia 1900–1950* (Stockholm 1957. 160 pp.)

HANS EPSTEIN: *Der Detektivroman der Unterschicht* (Frankfurt am Main 1930. 68 pp.)

GERARD FAIRLIE: *With Prejudice* (London 1952. 255 pp.)

BERNARD DE FALLOIS: *Simenon* (Paris 1961. 308 pp.)

FRANCOIS FOSCA: *Historie et technique du roman policier* (Paris 1937. 228 pp.)

RICHARD GANT: *Ian Fleming, The Man With the Golden Pen* (London 1966. 172 pp.)

GEBERS KRIMINALNYHETER. *Årgang 1–6 (1950–1955)* (Stockholm 1950–55).

WALTER GERTEIS: *Detektive. Ihre Geschichte im Leben und in der Literatur* (Munich 1953. 187 pp.)

MICHAEL GILBERT (ed.): *Crime in Good Company* (London 1959. 242 pp.)

O. F. GRAZEBROOK: *Studies in Sherlock Holmes 1–6* (Worcester 1950–51. 58, 38, 38, 32, 30 and 24 pp.)

ROGER LANCELYN GREEN: *A. E. W. Mason* (London 1952. 272 pp.)

GRAHAM GREENE & DOROTHY GLOVER: *Victorian Detective Fiction. A catalogue of the collection made by Dorothy Glover and Graham Greene* (London 1966. 151 pp.)

HUGH GREENE (ed.): *The Rivals of Sherlock Holmes* (London 1970. 352 pp.)

ORDEAN A. HAGEN: *Who Done It? A guide to detective,mystery and suspense fiction* (New York 1969. 834 pp.)

TREVOR H. HALL: *Sherlock Holmes. Ten literary studies* (London 1969. 157 pp.)

MICHAEL & MOLLIE HARDWICK: *The Sherlock Holmes Companion* (London 1962. 232 pp.)

MICHAEL & MOLLIE HARDWICK: *The Man Who Was Sherlock Holmes* (London 1964. 92 pp.)

RALPH HARPER: *The World of the Thriller* (Cleveland 1969. 140 pp.)

MICHAEL HARRISON: *Peter Cheyney, Prince of Hokum* (London 1954. 303 pp.)

MICHAEL HARRISON: *In the Footsteps of Sherlock Holmes* (London 1958. 292 pp.)

HOWARD HAYCRAFT: *Murder for Pleasure. The life and times of the detective story* (New York 1941. 409 pp. English edition with a foreword by Nicholas Blake, 1942. A supplementary chapter, *Notes on Additions to a Cornerstone Library*, is to be found in 'Ellery Queen's Mystery Magazine', October 1951, pp. 67–79.)

HOWARD HAYCRAFT (ed.): *The Art of the Mystery Story. A collection of critical essays* (New York 1946. 545 pp. Also published in Grosset's Universal Library 1961. 565 pp.)

A. D. HENRIKSEN: *221B Baker Street. Sherlock Holmes' privatliv* (Copenhagen 1949. 63 pp.)

A. D. HENRIKSEN (ed.): *Sherlock Holmes årbog* (Copenhagen 1965–).

PATRICIA HIGHSMITH: *Plotting and Writing Suspense Fiction* (Boston 1966. 149 pp.)

BASIL HOGARTH: *Writing Thrillers for Profit* (London 1936. 159 pp.)

JAMES EDWARD HOLROYD: *Baker Street By-Ways. A book about Sherlock Holmes* (London 1959. 159 pp.)

JAMES EDWARD HOLROYD (ed.): *Seventeen Steps to 221B.* (London 1967. 182 pp.)

FEREYDOUN HOVEYDA: *Petite histoire du roman policier* (Paris 1956. 95 pp.)

H. JACKSON: *About Edwin Drood* (Cambridge 1911. 90 pp.)

ALVA JOHNSTON: *The Case of Erle Stanley Gardner* (New York 1947. 87 pp.)

MARY KAVANAGH: *A New Solution of the Mystery of Edwin Drood* (London 1919. 32 pp.)

WALTER KLINEFELTER: *Sherlock Holmes in Portrait and Profile* (Syracuse, N.Y. 1963. 104 pp.)

LORENTZ N. KVAM: *Om norsk kriminallitteratur* (Oslo 1942. 20 pp.)

TAGE LA COUR: *Mord i biblioteket* (Stockholm 1953. 83 pp.)

TAGE LA COUR: *Studier i rødt. Causerier om kriminallitteratur* (Copenhagen 1956. 139 pp.)

TAGE LA COUR: *Mord med moral – og uden* (Copenhagen 1963. 51 pp.)

JOHN LAMOND: *Arthur Conan Doyle* (London 1931. 310 pp.)

MARGARET LANE: *Edgar Wallace* (London 1938. 423 pp. Revised edition with a foreword by Graham Greene, 1964. 338 pp.)

SHELDON LANE (ed.): *For Bond Lovers Only* (London 1965. 175 pp.)

ANDREW LANG: *The Puzzle of Dickens's Last Plot* (London 1905. 100 pp.)

HENRY LAURITSEN: *Sherlock Holmes løser Edwin Drood gåden* (Silkeborg 1964. 76 pp.)

C. DAY LEWIS (= Nicholas Blake): *The Buried Day* (London 1960. 244 pp.)

ALFRED LICHTENSTEIN: *Der Kriminalroman. Eine Literarische und vorensisch-medizinische Studie* (Munich 1908. 61 pp.)

PHILIP LINDSAY: *The Haunted Man. A portrait of Edgar Allan Poe* (London 1953. 256 pp.)

EDMOND LOCARD: *Policiers de roman et policiers de laboratoire* (Paris 1924. 274 pp.)

W. O. G. LOFTS & DEREK ADLEY: *The British Bibliography of Edgar Wallace.* Preface by Leslie Charteris (London 1969. 246 pp.)

H. LUDLAM: *A Bibliography of Dracula. The life story of Bram Stoker* (London 1962. 200 pp.)

BO LUNDIN: *Mordets enkla konst. Stencil för tvåbetygsseminarium* (Lund 1965. 21 pp.)

G. F. MCCLEARY: *On Detective Fiction and Other Things* (London 1960. 161 pp.)

CECIL MADDEN (ed.): *Meet the Detective* (London 1935. 143 pp.)

DAVID MADDEN (ed.): *Tough Guy Writers of the Thirties* (Carbondale 1968. 247 pp.)

MADEMOISELLE *Special mystery issue* (July 1964. 108 pp.)

NGAIO MARSH: *Black Beech and Honeydew. An autobiography* (London 1966. 287 pp.)

REGIS MESSAC: *Le 'detective novel' et l'influence de la pensée scientifique* (Paris 1929. 698 pp.)

MORD SOM HOBBY. *Specialnummer av tidskriften OBS* (1955:2.)

NIGEL MORLAND: *How to Write Detective Novels* (London 1936. 76 pp.)

A. E. MURCH: *The Development of the Detective Novel* (London 1958. 272 pp.)

MURDER IN ALBEMARLE STREET. *Catalogue from an exhibition of crime books, fact and fiction* (London 1962. 18 pp.)

MURDER MANUAL. *A handbook for mystery writers.* Introduction by H. F. Wight (East San Diego, Calif. 1936. 120 pp.)

THOMAS NARCEJAC: *Esthétique du roman policier* (Paris 1947. 201 pp.)

THOMAS NARCEJAC: *La fin d'un bluff. Essai sur le roman policier noir américain* (Paris 1949. 178 pp.)

THOMAS NARCEJAC: *Le cas Simenon* (Paris 1950. 191 pp. English edition, *The Art of Simenon*, London 1952.)

W. ROBERTSON NICOLL: *The Problem of 'Edwin Drood'* (London 1912. 212 pp.)

WILLIAM F. NOLAN: *Dashiell Hammett.* Introduction by Philip Durham (Santa Barbara 1969. 189 pp.)

PIERRE NORDON: *Sir Arthur Conan Doyle. L'homme et l'oeuvre* (Paris 1964. 481 pp. Abridged English edition, *Conan Doyle*, London 1966.)

JOHN O'CONNOR: *Father Brown on Chesterton* (London 1937. 173 pp.)

BARONESS (EMMUSKA) ORCZY: *Links in the Chain of Life* (London 1945. 223 pp.)

PAGING CRIME! *A catalogue from an exhibition of current books of crime fact and fiction. National Book League.* (London 1965. 27 pp.)

ORLANDO PARK: *Sherlock Holmes, Esq., and John H. Watson, M.D. An encyclopedia of their affairs* (Evanston Ill. 1962. 205 pp.)

HESKETH PEARSON: *Conan Doyle. His life and art* (London 1943. 194 pp.)

JOHN PEARSON: *The Life of Ian Fleming* (London 1966. 352 pp.)

ANTOINETTE PESKE & PIERRE MARTY: *Les terribles (Maurice Leblanc, Gaston Leroux, Marcel Allain)* (Paris 1951. 193 pp.)

POE-KLUBBENS ÅRBOG. (Copenhagen (1965–).

LES POLICIERS. *Le Bulletin du livre 108, 15 janvier 1964* (Paris 1964. 79 pp.)

REGINALD POUND: *The Strand Magazine 1891–1950.* (London 1966. 200 pp.)

ERIK POUPLIER (ed.): *Ti kriminelle minutter* (Copenhagen 1966. 47 pp.)

ELLERY QUEEN: *The Detective Short Story. A bibliography* (Boston 1942. 146 pp.)

ELLERY QUEEN: *Queen's Quorum* (Boston 1951. 132 pp.)

ELLERY QUEEN: *In the Queen's Parlor and Other Leaves from the Editor's Notebook* (New York 1957. 197 pp.)

(ELLERY QUEEN). *An Exhibition on the Occasion of the Opening of the Ellery Queen Collection. A catalogue from the Research of the University of Texas* (Austin 1959. 27 pp.)

ELLERY QUEEN & TAGE LA COUR: *Med venlig hilsen fra Ellery Queen* (Copenhagen 1958. 55 pp.)

G. C. RAMSAY: *Agatha Christie, Mistress of Mystery* (New York 1967. 138 pp.)

JOHN RAYMOND: *Simenon in Court. A Study* (London 1968. 193 pp.)

RED HERRINGS. *News Bulletin of the Crime Writers' Association* (London 1956–).

J. GUSTAF RICHERT: *Detektiven i romanen och verkligheten* (Stockholm 1928, 209 pp.)

MARY ROBERTS RINEHART: *My Story* (New York 1931. 432 pp.)

QUWNTIN RITZEN: *Simenon, avocat des hommes* (Paris 1961. 208 pp.)

S. C. ROBERTS: *Doctor Watson* (London 1931. 32 pp.)

S. C. ROBERTS: *Holmes and Watson* (London 1953. 138 pp.)

KENNETH ROBINSON: *Wilkie Collins* (London 1951. 348 pp.)

MARIE F. RODELL: *Mystery Fiction. Theory and technique* (New York 1943. 230 pp. English edition with a foreword by Maurice Richardson, London 1954.)

P. A. RUBER & WILLIAM SWIFT DALLIBA: *The Detective Short Story (a bibliography)* (New York 1961. 15 pp.)

JAMES SANDOE: *The Hard-boiled Dick. A personal check-list* (Chicago 1952. 10 pp.)

MONTAGU SAUNDERS: *The Mystery in the Drood Family* (Cambridge 1914. 160 pp.)

ARTHUR SCHIMMELPFENNING: *Beiträge zur Geschichte des Kriminalromans* (Dresden 1908. 16 pp.)

SUTHERLAND SCOTT: *Blood in Their Ink. The march of the modern mystery novel* (London 1953. 200 pp.)

EDGAR W. SMITH: *Baker Street Inventory, A Sherlockian bibliography* (Summit, N.J. 1945. 93 pp.)

EDGAR W. SMITH: *Sherlock Holmes, the Writings of John H. Watson, M.D. Late of the Army Medical Department (pseud. A. Conan Doyle) A bibliography of the sixty tales* (Morristown, N.J. 1962. 120 pp.)

EDGAR W. SMITH (ed.): *Profile by Gaslight. An irregular reader about the private life of Sherlock Holmes* (New York 1944. 312 pp.)

O. F. SNELLING: *Double O Seven. James Bond, a report* (London 1964. 160 pp.)

ROBERT STANDISH: *The Prince of Storytellers. The life of E. Phillips Oppenheim* (London 1957. 253 pp.)

VINCENT STARRETT: *The Private Life of Sherlock Holmes* (New York 1923. 214 pp. Revised edition, Chicago 1960.)

VINCENT STARRETT (ed.): *221B. Studies in Sherlock Holmes by Various Hands* (New York 1940. 248 pp.)

W. B. STEVENSON: *Detective Fiction. A reader's guide* (Cambridge 1949. 20 pp. Revised edition 1958. 32 pp.)

JULIAN SYMONS: *The Hundred Best Crime Stories* (London 1959. 21 pp.)

JULIAN SYMONS: *The Detective Story in Britain* (London 1962. 48 pp.)

WILLIAM TANNER: *The Book of Bond* (London 1965. 111 pp.)

THE THIRD DEGREE. *News Bulletin of the Mystery Writers of America* (New York 1945–).

GILBERT THOMAS: *How to Enjoy Detective Fiction* (London 1947. 108 pp.)

H. DOUGLAS THOMSON: *Masters of Mystery. A study of the detective story* (London 1931. 288 pp.)

THE TIMES LITERARY SUPPLEMENT. *Detective Fiction Number* (February 25, 1955). *Crime, Detection and Society* (June 23, 1961.)

TRIVIALLITTERATUR. *Aufsätze herausgegeben von Gerhard Schmidt-Henkel u. a. m.* (Berlin 1964. 266 pp.)

SIGURD TULLBERG: *O och A. Förteckning över detektivromaner på svenska språket utgivna 1901–1954* (Stockholm 1954. 95 pp.)

E. S. TURNER: *Boys Will Be Boys.* (London 1948. 269 pp. Revised edition, 1957. 277 pp.)

RICHARD USBORNE: *Clubland Heroes. A nostalgic study of some recurrent characters in the romantic fiction of Dornford Yates, John Buchan and Sapper* (London 1953. 217 pp.)

VIOLET WALLACE: *Edgar Wallace* (London 1932. 217 pp.)

JOHN WALSH: *Poe the Detective. The curious circumstances behind The Mystery of Marie Rogêt* (New Brunswick, N.J. 1968. 156 pp.)

CAROLYN WELLS: *The Technique of the Mystery Story* (Springfield, Mass. 1912. 336 pp. Revised edition 1929. 435 pp.)

J. N. WILLIAMSON: *A Critical History and Analysis of the 'Whodunit'.* (Indianapolis 1951. 26 pp.)

THOMAS WÜRTENBERGER: *Die deutsche Kriminalerzählung* (Erlangen 1941. 40 pp.)

FRITZ WÖLCKEN: *Der literarische Mord. Eine Untersuchung über die englische und amerikanische Detektivliteratur* (Nuremberg 1953. 348 pp.)

HENRY A. ZEIGER: *Ian Fleming, the Spy Who Came In with the Gold* (New York 1965. 158 pp.)

More crime books worth reading

MARTHA ALBRAND
USA. Best known for spy and agent novels, e.g. *A Door Fell Shut, Nightmare in Copenhagen, No Surrender, A Day in Monte Carlo* and *Call from Austria.*

JOHN BALL
USA. Created the negro detective, Virgil Tibbs: *In The Heat of the Night* and *The Cool Cottontail.*

CHRISTIANNA BRAND
UK. Detective novels, e.g. *London Particular, Green for Danger, Heads You Lose* and *Cat and Mouse.*

CHARLOTTE ARMSTRONG
USA. Psychological thrillers, e.g. *Mischief, A Little Less Than Kind, The Witch's House* and a collection of short stories, *The Albatross.*

JEFFREY ASHFORD
UK. Crime novels, e.g. *Hands of Innocence, Counsel for the Defence* and *Investigations are Proceeding.*

JOSEPHINE BELL
UK. Detective novels, e.g. *Murder in Hospital* (a favourite theme), *Bones in the Barrow* and *The Upfold Witch.*

ANDERS BODELSEN
Denmark. Two psychological novels: *Tænk På et tal* and *Hændeligt uheld.*

JOHN BINGHAM
UK. Originally crime, later spy novels, e.g. *My Name is Michael Sibley, Five Roundabouts to Heaven, Murder Plan Six* and *A Fragment of Fear.*

FREDRIC BROWN
USA. Thrillers – with splendid short stories in the collection *The Shaggy Dog* – and novels such as *Murder Can Be Fun, The Screaming Mimi* and *The Wench is Dead.*

VICTOR CANNING
UK. Agent and smuggling novels, etc., e.g. *Venetian Bird, House of the Seven Flies* and *The Scorpio Letters.*

FRANCIS DIDELOT

France. Psychological crime novels: *Le eptième jure* and *Nuit après nuit;* detective novels, e.g. the series featuring Commissioner Bignon.

FRANCIS CLIFFORD

UK. Spy and agent novels, e.g. *The Trembling Earth, The Naked Runners* and *All Men Are Lonely Now.*

KERSTIN EKMAN

Sweden. Detective novels, e.g. *30 Meter mord, Den brinnande ugnen* and *Dödsklockan.*

ROALD DAHL

Cosmopolitan. Known especially for his collections of short story thrillers, *Someone Like You* and *Kiss, Kiss.*

HELEN EUSTIS

USA. Famous for the psychological thriller, *The Horizontal Man.*

JAMES HADLEY CHASE

UK. Hard-boiled thrillers by the dozen, e.g. *No Orchids for Miss Blandish.*

JAN EKSTRÖM

Sweden. Detective novels, e.g. *Döden går i moln, Träfracken, Morianerna* and *Älkistan.*

ELSE FISCHER

Denmark. Crime novels, e.g. *Telefonen er afbrudt, Huset i lyngbakkerne* and *Døden står på ski;* and the thriller, *Portrætternes hus.*

CELIA FREMLIN
UK. Psychological thrillers, e.g. *The Hours Before Dawn, The Jealous One* and *Prisoner's Base*.

EDMUND CRISPIN
UK. Detective novels, e.g. *The Moving Toyshop, Love Lies Bleeding* and *Frequent Hearses.*

DICK FRANCIS
UK. Detective novels from the racecourse, e.g. *Dead Cert, Odds Against* and *Flying Finish*.

STANLEY ELLIN
USA. Thrillers such as *Dreadful Summit* and *The Eighth Circle* and collections of short stories, e.g. *Mystery Stories* and *The Blessington Method.*

MICHAEL GILBERT
UK. Detective novels, e.g. *Smallbone Deceased* and *The Crack in the Teacup*

EDWARD GRIERSON
UK. Crime novels, the best known being *Reputation for a Song* and *The Second Man.*

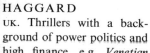

WILLIAM HAGGARD
UK. Thrillers with a background of power politics and high finance, e.g. *Venetian Blind, The Unquiet Sleep* and *The Powder Barrel*.

MOGENS MUGGE HANSEN
Denmark. Detective novels: *Hvem myrdede frk. klædeskab, Marselisborgmordet* and *Døden spiser med pinde.*

ADAM HALL
(Elleston Trevor)
UK. Crime and spy novels, e.g, *The Billboard Madonna, The Shoot* and *The Berlin Memorandum.*

MICHAEL INNES
UK. Detective novels, e.g. *Hamlet Revenge, Lament for a Maker, The Man from the Sea* and *The Journeying Boy*.

SÉBASTIEN JAPRISOT
France. A detective novel, *Compartiment tueurs* and psychological thrillers, e.g. *Piège pour Cendrillon* and *La Dame dans l'auto avec des lunettes et un fusil*.

HELGE HAGERUP
Norway. The crime novel *Et stikk i hjertet* and many short stories.

JAMES LEASOR
UK. Spy novels: *Passport to Oblivion, Passport to Peril, Passport in Suspense* and *Passport for a Pilgrim*.

HARRY KEMELMAN
USA. The rabbi detective David Small in *Friday the Rabbi Slept Late* and *Saturday the Rabbi went Hungry*.

GAVIN LYALL
UK. Thrillers: *The Most Dangerous Game, Midnight Plus One, Shooting Script* and *The Wrong Side of the Sky*.

EDGAR LUSTGARTEN
UK. Trial court novels, e.g. *A Case to Answer*.

RUFUS KING
USA. A detective novel *Murder by the Clock* and collections of short stories: *Malice in Wonderland, The Steps to Murder* and *The Faces of Danger*.

ROSS
MACDONALD
USA. Detective novels, e.g. *The Moving Target, The Zebra-Striped Hearse, The Galton Case* and *The Far Side of the Dollar.*

HELEN MacINNES
UK. Spy and crime novels, e.g. *The Venetian Affair, Assignment in Brittany* and *The Double Image.*

PHILIP MacDONALD
UK. Detective novels, e.g. *The Rasp, The Noose* and *The Nursemaid Who Disappeared.*

WILLIAM
P. McGIVERN
USA. Police novels, e.g. *The Big Hat, Shield for Murder, Rogue Cop* and *The Seven File.*

DOROTHY B.
HUGHES
USA. Thrillers, e.g. *The So Blue Marble, The Blackbirder* and *In a Lonely Place.*

JOYCE PORTER
UK. Police novels about Inspector Dover.

HELEN McCLOY
USA. Crime novels, e.g. *Through a Glass Darkly* and *The One that Got Away.*

PATRICIA MOYES
Ireland. Crime novels, e.g. *Dead Men Don't Ski, Death on the Agenda, Murder à la Mode* and *Falling Star.*

GERD NYQUIST
Norway. Detective novels: *Avdøde ønsket ikke blomster* and *Stille som graven.*

ARTHUR OMRE
Norway. The crime novel *Mysterium i rolvsøy* (under the pseudonym Arthur Juel); criminal novels: *Smuglere* and *Flukten*; and many short stories.

FRANK RICHARD
(Hans Habe)
Germany. Courtroom novel *Die Frau des Staatsanwalts*.

MARGARET MILLAR
Canada. Thrillers, e.g. *A Beast in View* and *A Wall of Eyes*.

PATRICK QUENTIN
(Q. Patrick-Jonathan Stagge)
USA. Detective and crime novels, e.g. *S.S. Murder, The Man with Two Wives, The Grindle Nightmare, Murder of Mercy* and *The Black Widow*.

MAURICE PROCTER
UK. First British author to write police novels, e.g. *The Chief Inspector's Statement, Devil in Moonlight, Man in Ambush* and *Exercise Hoodwink*.

PETER SANDER
Denmark. Criminal novels: *Døden kommer til Middag* and (under the pseudonym Bengt J. Nielsen) *Blues for Kitty*.

CRAIG RICE
USA. Detective novels, e.g. *The Wrong Murder, Trial by Fury* and *Home Sweet Homicide*.

CLAYTON RAWSON
USA. Detective novels and short stories about the conjurer, The Great Merlini, e.g. *Death from a Tophat* and *Death Walks on the Ceiling*.

OLE SARVIG
Denmark. Psychological criminal novels: *Havet under mit vindue* and *De Sovende*.

SEYMOUR SHUBIN
USA. The psychological thriller *A Stranger to Myself*.

JOSEPHINE TEY
UK. Crime novels in a variety of milieux, e.g. *The Franchise Affair, A Shilling for Candles, The Singing Sands* and *The Daughter of Time*.

MAJ SJÖWALL and PER WAHLÖÖ
Sweden. Police novels: *Roseanna, Mannen som gick upp i rök* and *Mannen på balkongen*.

MICHAEL GRUNDT SPANG

Norway. Criminal novels: *Den ukjente morder* (reportage), *En morder går løs* and *Operasjon v for vanvidd*.

REX STOUT

USA. Famous for his novels about the amateur detective Nero Wolfe, e.g. *The League of the Frightened Men, Some Buried Caesar, Fer-de-Lance* and *Before Midnight*.

HELLE STANGERUP

Denmark. Criminal novels: *Gravskrift for rødhætte* and *Gule handsker*.

CORNELL WOOLRICH (William Irish)

USA. Crime and detective novels and thrillers, e.g. *The Bride Wore Black, Phantom Lady* and *The Night I Died,* and a collection of short stories, *After-Dinner Story*.

HILLARY WAUGH

USA. Detective novels, e.g. *Last Seen Wearing, Pure Poison, Girl on the Run* and *End of a Party*.

MIKA WALTARI

Finland. Police novels: *Vem mördade fru kroll?* and *Mysteriet rygseck*.

MARY STEWART

UK. Thrillers, e.g. *Madam, Will You Talk?, My Brother Michael, This Rough Magic* and *The Gabriel Hounds*.

BENT THORNDAHL

Denmark. Criminal novels: *Mordet i poe-klubben* and *En bolighajs død*; special agent novel *Damen i rødt*.

Index

Picture copyrights

Page 11: Water-colour by Russell Hoban from Edgar Allan Poe: *Tales and Poems*. The Macmillan Company, 1963. By permission of the publishers. Page 18: Drawing from Edogawa Rampo: *Japanese Tales of Mystery and Imagination*. Illustrated by M. Kuwata. Charles E. Tuttle, 1956. By permission of the publishers. Page 19: Coloured drawing from Leon Comber: *The Strange Cases of Magistrate Pao. Chinese tales of crime and detection*. Illustrated by Lo Koon-Chiu. Charles E. Tuttle, 1964. By permission of the publishers. Page 23: Illustration by Majeska from Isak Dinesen: *Seven Gothic Tales*, Random House Inc., 1934. By permission of the publishers. Page 37: Strip cartoon from The Moonstone No. 30 by permission of the publishers, Classics Illustrated, 101 Fifth Avenue, New York. Page 39: Drawings by Charles Huard from *Oeuvres complètes de Balzac*. By permission of Librairie de l'Abbaye, Paris. Page 49: Drawing by Ronald Searle. By permission of the artist. Page 50: All illustrations by Frederic Dorr Steele. By kind permission of Mrs William A. Grey, Connecticut. Page 59: Illustration by Stanley L. Wood from Guy Boothby: *Doctor Nikola*, 4th edition. Ward, Lock & Co., 1897. By permission of the publishers. Page 60: Illustration from K. & Hesketh Prichard: *The Chronicles of Don Q*. Illustrated by Stanley L. Wood. Chapman & Hall, 1904. By permission of Associated Book Publishers Ltd, London. Page 67: Photo by O. J. Morris from Michael Harrison: *In the Footsteps of Sherlock Holmes*, originally published in O. J. Morris: *Grandfather's London*. By permission of Putnam & Company, London. Page 68: From R. L. Stevenson: *The Strange Case of Dr Jekyll and Mr Hyde*. Illustrated by S. G. Hulme Beaman. John Lane, 1930. By permission of The Bodley Head, London. Page 73: Illustration by Cyrus Cuneo from Baroness Orczy: *Lady Molly of Scotland Yard*. Cassell & Co., 1910. By permission of the

publishers. Page 74: Illustration by Lucius Hitchcock from Mark Twain: *A Double-Barrelled Detective Story*. Harper & Brothers, 1902. By permission of the publishers. Page 76: Illustration by Rea Irvin from Ellis Parker Butler: *Philo Gubb, Correspondence-School Detective*. Houghton Mifflin, 1918. By permission of the publishers. Page 77: Drawing by Charles Beck from Jacques Futrelle: *The Thinking Machine*. Copyright: Scholastic Magazines, Inc., New York. Page 80: Illustration by Edward Read from Guy Boothby: *A Prince of Swindlers*. Ward, Lock & Co., 1897. By permission of the publishers. Page 80: From George Randolph Chester: *Young Wallingford*. Copyright: 1910, The Bobbs-Merrill Company Inc.; 1938, Mrs George Randolph Chester. By permission of the publishers. Page 85: Caricature by Max Beerbohm from Roger Lancelyn Green: *A. E. W. Mason*. Max Parrish, London, 1952. By permission of the publishers. Page 91: Illustration by Cyrus Cuneo from E. W. Hornung: *A Thief in the Night*. Chatto and Windus, 1905. By permission of the publishers. Page 92: Illustrations by H. M. Brock from R. Austin Freeman: *John Thorndyke's Cases*. Chatto and Windus, 1909. By permission of the publishers. Page 94: Illustration by Fred Pegram from Clifford Ashdown: *The Adventures of Romney Pringle*. 'Cassell's Magazine (London)', June-November 1902. By permission of the publishers. Page 95: Illustration by Will Foster from Arthur B. Reeve: *The Silent Bullet. The Adventures of Craig Kennedy, Scientific Detective*. Dodd, Mead & Co., 1912. By permission of the publishers. Pages 97–8: Illustrations by Sidney Seymour Lucas from G. K. Chesterton: *The Wisdom of Father Brown*. Cassell & Co., 1914. By permission of the publishers. Page 99: Illustration by the author from G. K. Chesterton: *The Club of Queer Trades*. By permission of Cassell & Co. Ltd, London. Page 102: Stills from *The Lodger* with Merle Oberon and George Sanders.

20th Century Fox, 1944. By permission of the film company. Page 108: Portrait of Poirot by W. Smithson Broadhead from G. C. Ramsey: *Agatha Christie, Mistress of Mystery*. Dodd, Mead & Co., 1967. By permission of L.E.A., London. Page 109: Cover picture from Agatha Christie: *The Mysterious Affair at Styles*. Pan Books Ltd. By permission of the publishers. Page 112: Copyright: C. A. Pearson Ltd, London. Pages 128–9: Raymond Chandler photos by permission of University of California, Photographic Department, Los Angeles. Page 143: Photo by Irving Penn from *Augenblicke*. Copyright: 1951, The Condé Nast Publications Inc. Pages 144–5: Copyright: 1937, Detective Comics, Inc.; renewed 1964, National Periodical Publications, Inc. All Rights Reserved. Page 146: Illustration by Gerhard M. Hotop from Balduin Groller: *Dagobert Trostler*. Henry Goverts Verlag GmbH, Stuttgart, 1967. Page 146: Photo by Gilda Kuhlman from Jorge Luis Borges: *Labyrinths. Selected stories and other writings*. New Direction, 1962. By permission of the photographer. Page 155: Illustration by Albert Levering from John Kendrick Bangs: *Mrs Raffles. Being the adventures of an amateur crackswoman*. Harper & Brothers, 1905. By permission of the publishers. Page 155: Drawing by Herb Roth from Ebenezer Murgatroyd: *Cooking to Kill. The Poison Cook Book*. Peter Pauper Press, 1951. By permission of the publishers. Page 157: Drawing by Tom Walker from Jan Broberg: *Deckarens début och dilemma*. By permission of 'Council of Four', Denver, Colorado. Page 161: Painting by Amherst Villiers from Ian Fleming: *On Her Majesty's Secret Service*. Jonathan Cape, 1963. By permission of the artist. Page 167: Cover picture to Patricia Highsmith: *The Cry of the Owl*. Pan Books Ltd. By permission of the publishers. Page 168: Drawing by Vlaminck. By permission of S.P.A.D.E.M., Paris.

Triumph of God's Revenge,
The 21
Trois Crimes D'Arsène
Lupin, Les 88
Trostler, Dagobert 146
Trygon Factor, The 114
Träpracken 151
Twain, Mark (pseudonym),
see Clemens, Samuel L.
Twelve Mystery Stories 112

U
Uncle Abner 134, 135
Uncle Gavin 135
Under the Sunset 59
Union Jack, The 79
Unique Hamlet, The 54
Unpopular Opinions 113
Unravelled Knots 76
Upfield, Arthur W. 146
Utterson, Mr 68

V
Valk, Piet van der 153

Valley of Fear, The 46, 57
Vance, Philo 132
Van Dine, S. S. (pseudo-
nym), see Wright, Willard
Huntington
Van Dusen, Augustus
S. F. X. 76
Vautrin, 38
Vem av de sju 151
Verdict of Twelve 139
Vickers, Roy (alias
Durham, David) 81, 94,
143
Vidocq, Eugène François
38
Vivild, Niels 67
Voltaire, François 63

W
Wagner, Peter 60
Wahlöö, Per 151, 184
Wallace, Edgar 43, 81, 114,
115
Wallingford, Get-Rich-
Quick 81

Walpole, Horace 22
Waltari, Mika 185
Wandering Jew, The 40
Warner, Warren 136
Warrender, Mrs 73
Waters 21
Watson, Dr John H. 46–52,
54–57, 106
Waugh, Hillary 185
Wells, H. G. 58
West, Roger 153
Wheatley, Dennis 120
Wheeler, Simon 132
Wijk, Christer 150
Wilkins, Mary E. 100
William Wilson 11
Willis, Inspector 107
Wimsey, Lord Peter 97,
112, 113
Wisdom of Father Brown,
The 97
With My Little Eye 104,
105
Withers, Hildegarde 63, 73
Witness for the Prosecution
137

Woman in White, The 35
Woolrich, Cornell (pseudonym of Irish, William)
185
Wright, Willard Hunting-
don (alias Van Dine, S. S.)
121, 132, 133
Wu T'se Chin An 16

Y
Yates, Dornford 82
You Only Live Twice 163
Young Wallingford 81
Yours Truly, Jack the Ripper
100

Z
Zadig 63
Zangwill, Israel 42, 140, 141
Zimmertür, Dr 95, 150